Chesapeake and Ohio Canal

A Guide to Chesapeake and
Ohio Canal National Historical Park
Maryland, District of Columbia,
and West Virginia

D1359237

Produced by the
Division of Publications
National Park Service

U.S. Department of the Interior
Washington, D.C. 1991

Using This Handbook
Chesapeake and Ohio Canal National Historical
Park is a unit of the National Park System, which
consists of more than 350 parks representing important examples of our country's natural and cultural
inheritance. This park preserves one of the Nation's
most intact historic canals. It also fortuitously protects part of the Potomac River valley as a natural,
historical, and recreational resource of inestimable
value. This handbook is published in support of the
National Park Service's management policies and
interpretive programs at the park. Part 1 places the
park in its historical setting—the 19th-century canal
era—and tells how citizen initiative eventually saved
it from highway building. Part 2 explains how the
canal was built, how it worked, who made it work,
and what it contributed to developing agriculture,
mining, and industry in the Potomac River basin.
Part 3 presents concise travel guide information,
detailed canal maps, and other reference materials to
help you make the most of a visit to the canal.

Part 1

Welcome to the C&O Canal

A Flatwater Route to Western Wealth

Pages 2-3: *Lights from Harpers Ferry penetrate mists hovering above the confluence of the Shenandoah and Potomac rivers. The C&O Canal worked westward here, hugging the wall of Maryland Heights at right.*

Pages 4-5: *No longer lived in, a squared-log lockhouse still keeps a watchful eye on its lock chamber. Most lockhouses were built of stone or brick.*

Today's superhighway construction, sprawling towns, and fast inland transport make it hard to appreciate what impact the Chesapeake and Ohio Canal had on isolated rural and village folk from Washington, D.C., to Cumberland, Maryland, in the mid-1800s. Penetrating 185 miles inland, the C&O Canal was one of the Nation's most ambitious industrial experiments of the time.

In 1800 barely one million people lived west of the Allegheny Mountains, but by 1830 this region held some 3.5 million people, nearly a quarter of the total population. The burning desire of eastern merchants and port cities was to tap the region's resources and markets. Their desire fueled the drive for internal improvements westward. The immediate goal was to tap the Ohio River trade. The National Road had reached the Ohio at Wheeling, Virginia (now West Virginia), in 1818, carrying much traffic. However, moving goods by road in those days was arduous and more than 30 times more expensive than flatwater canal transport. Contemporary calculations demonstrated that in one day four horses could draw a one-ton payload by wagon 12 miles over ordinary roads. On turnpikes four horses could draw a one-and-a-half-ton payload 18 miles. On flatwater canals, however, the same four horses could transport 100 tons 24 miles per day. The savings and efficiency meant that bulky products could go to market more profitably.

Looking back, canals of the period made roads of that day obsolete, but many canals were in turn made obsolete by railroads. On July 4, 1828, President John Quincy Adams turned the first shovelful of dirt on the canal. On that very day Marylander Charles Carroll was similarly launching construction of the Baltimore and Ohio Railroad in Baltimore, Maryland. The railroad beat the canal to the Cumberland coalfields and soon reached the Ohio River, but the canal was never completed beyond Cumberland.

President Adams' shovel struck roots, then rocks, symbolizing the obstacles that would confront the canal builder. The ordinarily stiff and formal President took off his jacket, rolled up his sleeves, and tried again. The Fourth of July crowd cheered. President Adams would call this the greatest moment of his life. He had begun a project that would cost investors $14 million, a sum that represented then the same percentage of Gross National Product the Federal Government would one day spend to put a man on the moon. As you jog, backpack, or bike the towpath from Cumberland to Washington today, the cost strikes you as a bargain many times over.

The C&O Canal was heir to a fond dream of George Washington when it assumed the charter of Washington's Patowmack Company, which began its work in 1785. George Washington had sought to make the Potomac River navigable to the West and the Ohio River valley by constructing skirting canals around falls, rapids, and other impediments to navigation. Even before the end of the Revolutionary War, Washington knew the promise of the West. He had acquired his first western lands, in the Shenandoah Valley, as a teenager in 1750. He had been granted 15,000 acres of Ohio land as military bounty at the close of the French and Indian Wars and then purchased as much from fellow officers. After the Revolutionary War the fledgling Nation joined George Washington in looking westward to tap the region's wealth of furs and timber, to settle its lands for agriculture, and to vie for control of the lucrative Mississippi River trade. In addition, France, Spain, and England still loomed as competitors to the West.

In the United States, as in Europe, the greatest obstacle to industrial development was poor internal transportation. The needs of industry would, in fact, usher in the canal era on both sides of the Atlantic. Industrialization required the gathering of quantities of often bulky raw materials and then the

distribution of manufactured goods far and wide. Could the developing United States of America orchestrate the logistics these large enterprises would require?

The Revolution had had little effect on the Potomac Valley and the wilderness sprawling beyond it. Trails existed through the towering hardwoods that grew so closely together that their shade kept the forest floor clear of undergrowth. Rough trails on uneven floors of the dense forest were passable only for people on foot or on horseback. Despite shallows, treacherous rapids, and arduous portages around Little and Great Falls, the Potomac River itself was the main highway. For settling the West and the Potomac Valley, the river would have to be made navigable.

In the spring of 1785, Elkanah Watson, a young man who had spent the past five years studying the canal systems of Europe, captured Washington's imagination at Mount Vernon. He urged Washington to improve the Potomac River by using canals to bypass its difficult parts. At the 1785 Mount Vernon Convention, Washington and other delegates from Maryland and Virginia discussed improving the upper Potomac and constructing a road from the "head of navigation to the waters running into the Ohio" near present-day Wheeling.

As Watson left Mount Vernon, Washington was convinced that his desires were fully practical. That same year he became first president of the Patowmack Company, which was chartered in both Virginia and Maryland to make the river navigable from tidewater to the western limits and to improve the tributaries for navigation.

The chain of locks that the Patowmack Company blasted through solid rock on the Virginia side of the river at Great Falls best memorializes Washington's first practical push westward. Completed in 1802, the locks, still visible at Great Falls Park, were widely described in European technical journals as engineering feats of their time. With three skirting canals around rapids at Harpers Ferry, Seneca, and Little Falls, the Great Falls skirting canal rendered 218 miles of the Potomac navigable. By using the company's canals, channels, buoys, grappling chains, and anchoring rings, boatmen in keel boats could thwart an undependable river. At spring high water a keel boat could go the 197 river miles from Cumberland to George-

George Washington founded the Patowmack Company in 1785 to improve Potomac River navigation.

Facing page: *Crews costumed in canal era garb offer today's visitors boat rides at Georgetown and Great Falls. The trips include passage through locks at those locations and are often accompanied by songs popular during the canal's heyday.*

Canal system in 1850

Reaching its peak in the 1850s in the United States, the canal era then boasted some 4,000 miles of canals, most of which are abandoned today. This map is redrawn from work by Richard C. Waugh, Jr., in Best of American Canals.

Facing page: *Leaks in a lock gate create a cascade whose simple music offers refreshment to pedestrians bustling about Georgetown's commercial area today.*

town in perhaps four days. But danger abounded: boatmen often navigated at flood stage stretches of river today considered unsafe for power boats. Nevertheless, in one year of record, 1,300 boats 60 to 65 feet long and 8 feet wide and with cargo capacities up to 15 tons made the run from Cumberland to Georgetown or Washington, D.C.

Despite its great social and economic importance to life in the Potomac watershed, hazards and other shortcomings of the Patowmack Company's canals were soon apparent. However, it was not until work commenced on New York State's Erie Canal, in 1817, that Maryland and Virginia moved to seriously investigate an all-canal route that would offer dependable navigation for most of the year between Washington and the Ohio River's link with the Mississippi. By 1823, meetings of delegates from Virginia, Maryland, and Pennsylvania were being held to plan for such a canal and to interest the Federal Government in the project. With the growing success of the Erie Canal, enthusiasm mounted for the C&O Canal as a flatwater route to western wealth.

The Erie, completed in 1825, stretched 363 miles from Buffalo to Albany, linking the Hudson River with Lake Erie and thereby connecting the seaboard with the interior. In 1817 New York City was isolated at the Hudson River's mouth. City merchants watched helplessly as Midwest farmers shipped their products down the Ohio and Mississippi rivers to far distant New Orleans and as Midwest merchants imported goods over improved roads from Philadelphia and Baltimore. Meanwhile, the rise of steamboat shipping on the Mississippi posed even darker threats to New York's coastal trade. New York State's own southwestern counties shipped their grain and timber by flatboat to Pittsburgh via the Allegheny River or to Baltimore via the Susquehanna; Lake Ontario districts traded with Montreal via the St. Lawrence; and the Lake Champlain area shipped its iron, timber, and farm products into Canada by the Sorel or Richelieu rivers. Why? Because overland freight rates to New York City were horrendous: shipping one ton of goods from Buffalo to New York City cost $100. Shipping the same ton to Montreal would cost only $30—and a return freight would still cost only $60 to $75 per ton.

The Erie Canal so vastly altered shipping econom-

"Two Little Sisters"

"Cumberland Boatyard"

Recording every side of canal life, from intimate family scenes to the industry of a terminus town, the watercolors of John Louis Wellington (1878-1965) evoke the spirit of the canal era. He was a Cumberland native who in the early part of the century painted some 52 pictures along the C&O Canal.

"Train Over the Canal Terminus" (at Cumberland)

"Man and Woman Crossing a River Lock"

A boatman's lantern and horn provided basic communications between canal boats and the lockkeepers. The latter were on call round the clock to lock canal boats through.

ics that it restructured channels of commerce and transformed New York City into a world trade center and the preeminent U.S. entry point for immigrants. The distance between the Northwest and the sea was shorter by the Erie Canal than through either the Mississippi or St. Lawrence shipping networks. Overnight the freight rate from Buffalo to New York City dropped from $100 per ton to $10 or $12. The former 20-day trip was shortened to 8 days.

Unprecedented prosperity followed for a large portion of the United States. Also, passenger packets moved westward-bound settlers from Albany to Buffalo in just four and a half days. In the process the Erie Canal spurred further rapid development of farms and other economic ventures in the hinterlands that now fed New York's burgeoning port operations. A contemporary expressed it in largely justified superlatives: "They have built the longest canal in the world in the least time, with the least experience, for the least money, and to the greatest public benefit."

With the Erie Canal, New York City inherited George Washington's dream of a water transportation link between the West and the east coast. The Erie also established an important precedent that would further Washington's dream for a Potomac canal route: the Erie Canal was no mere private venture, but an enterprise of New York State. It therefore provided convincing practical demonstration of the efficacy of public support for the internal improvements desperately needed for our Nation's industrialization efforts. This internal improvements issue, strenuously debated following the Nation's founding, bore strongly on the prospects for the C&O Canal project.

President George Washington's treasury secretary, Alexander Hamilton, had demonstrated the advantages of federal involvement in transportation in his insightful "Report on Manufactures." Little attention was paid to his advocacy, except that Congress did authorize appropriations for a few lighthouses. Voices raised to advocate the federal construction of *internal* improvements generated little support. In 1806, however, Congress authorized the first surveys for the National Road, which was projected to run from Cumberland to St. Louis to tie the new areas with the seaboard states. In 1808, President Thomas Jefferson's secretary of the treasury, Albert Gallatin, presented to the Senate his report on "Roads and Canals," an early attempt to formulate a comprehensive plan of national improvements. Citing many impediments to such undertakings—including lack of private capital and sparse population patterns—Gallatin concluded that the "General Government can alone remove these obstacles." Furthermore, Gallatin wrote, "No other single operation, within the power of Government, can more effectually tend to strengthen and perpetuate that Union which secures external independence, domestic peace, and internal liberty." The War of 1812 halted momentum for committing public funds to internal improvements, however, and the National Road remained the one major enterprise constructed by the Federal Government during this period.

Return of peace in 1814 ushered in new economic development. The lack of internal navigation along the seacoast had hampered the U.S. Navy in the war, and the Army had been frustrated by transport problems on the Great Lakes. People no longer felt economically dependent on Britain and renewed their efforts to establish links between the agricultural West and the industrial East. Proponents of a Chesapeake and Ohio Canal took advantage of this national expansionist mood.

Determining that a navigable canal independent of the river was needed to provide for a direct water communication between the Potomac and Ohio Valleys, the states of Maryland, Virginia, and Pennsylvania chartered the Chesapeake and Ohio Canal Company in 1828 to build such a line. Construction was begun in July of that year under chief engineer Benjamin Wright, formerly chief engineer on the Erie Canal project. The canal was open to Seneca by 1831, to Harpers Ferry in 1834, to the Cacapon River above Hancock in 1839, and to Cumberland in 1850. At Cumberland it halted forever, having cost slightly more than $11,000,000. Construction was plagued by labor shortages and unrest, inadequate availability of construction materials, unforeseen difficulties relating to geography, short-lived federal support, constant funds shortages, and legal battles with the upstart Baltimore and Ohio Railroad. Railroads were unproven then, but locomotive power to pull heavy freight loads was soon developed. The dawn of the railroad age

Identified as Clint America Winchester, this workman sits atop a lockside snubbing post. Crews looped ropes around these stout posts to stabilize boats being raised or lowered in swirling lock waters. Boats that damaged lock masonry drew hefty fines. Note the deep rope burns at post bottom. Few if any original snubbing posts survive on the canal.

had a momentous impact on the C&O project.

Subject to frequent flooding, stiff B&O railroad competition, and Civil War conflicts, the canal turned profits only in the 1870s. After the devastating 1889 flood, the canal went into a receivership to the B&O Railroad, which would operate the canal until another severe flood, in 1924, caused the canal to be closed for good.

The canal was acquired by the Federal Government for $2 million in 1938 as a result of the financial difficulties experienced by the railroad during the Great Depression. It was placed under the National Park Service. After much soul-searching on what to do with it, the Park Service, with public support, proposed building a parkway for automobiles modeled after Skyline Drive and Blue Ridge Parkway. What more perfect roadbed than a level right-of-way already federally owned?

Although eminently practical, the road proposal turned out to be anathema to those who saw the canal environs as an antidote to the Potomac River Valley's rampant urbanization. In 1954, Associate Supreme Court Justice William O. Douglas challenged editors of *The Washington Post* and *The Evening Star* newspapers to walk the length of the canal with him to assess its beauty and historical significance. "One who walked the canal its full length could plead that cause with the eloquence of a John Muir," Douglas wrote to the newspapers. Two editors took up the challenge. Douglas, six fellow stalwarts, and the two editors completed the March 1954 hike of some 180 miles amidst much journalistic hoopla. Fifty thousand canal converts welcomed them at Georgetown. *The Washington Post* changed its editorial mind in favor of preserving the canal, and the property was saved by popular appeal.

Today the canal and its towpath with beautiful bordering forests and Potomac riverscapes attract legions of outdoor enthusiasts. *Canal Clipper* boaters, joggers, winter skaters, hikers, backpackers, rock climbers, boaters, canoeists, anglers, artists, philosophers, poets, and lovers all turn out in their respective seasons. In the tranquil company of history they revel in the green ribbon of natural wealth that is the serendipitous legacy—a renewing internal improvement—of this great national project.

Associate Supreme Court Justice William O. Douglas championed the preservation of the C&O Canal. He challenged pro-development news editors to walk its length with him in 1954. Because of the hike, The Washington Post *newspaper changed its editorial views. The canal would be preserved by popular acclaim. This bust of the late Justice Douglas was placed on the canal in Georgetown and dedicated in 1977.*

Facing page: *Its towpath now turned footpath, the C&O Canal provides a superbly natural walkway at the doorway of the Nation's Capital.*

Part 2

The Great National Project

The Construction Challenge

Preceding pages: *Dressed in garb of the canal era, a crewman for today's boat rides on the C&O Canal helps ease his long boat into a lock chamber. Ropes looped around stout snubbing posts kept canal boats from damaging the masonry as water levels in the lock chambers were raised or lowered.*

Groundbreaking ceremonies for the Chesapeake and Ohio Canal were held near the Powder Magazine at the head of Little Falls on July 4, 1828. The canal board asked President John Quincy Adams to turn the first spadeful of earth and invited many representatives of official Washington and foreign delegations to the ceremonies. The board and official guests breakfasted in Georgetown and then boated 5 miles upriver to the groundbreaking site. After several brief speeches, President Adams gave the project his Independence Day blessing, emphasized its national character, and, with several false starts occasioned by unfortunately rocky ground, turned the first spadeful of dirt. The official party then returned to Georgetown for a lavish dinner. The groundbreaking affair proved a grand success that focused public attention on the C&O Canal as a national project and completely overshadowed the inaugural ceremonies of the Baltimore and Ohio Railroad in Baltimore the same day.

Such a monumental engineering and construction challenge as that posed by the C&O Canal project in 1828 would be difficult to imagine today. Under its charter the canal company must build 100 miles of operable canal in five years. There were no construction firms to undertake such large-scale works. Schools of engineering would not come into existence for another 25 years; the only engineers available were practical engineers. Auspiciously, the canal board hired as chief engineer Benjamin Wright, who had served with great distinction in that capacity during construction of the Erie Canal. Before his Erie Canal experience, however, Wright's resume was that of a country lawyer who had also done some surveying. Wright *became* an engineer by practical experience, not by training. Canal-era historian Alvin Harlow observed that when the first canals in America were built ". . . there was not a native-born engineer in America, and almost none of any nationality."

Researching the canal's archival records you might expect to find detailed engineering drawings, but there are only written specifications and detailed material lists that are accompanied by rudimentary sketches. What is more, the 184.5-mile canal was built in multiple sections that averaged only a half mile in length. This immense task was accomplished by independent contractors working in an overwhelmingly rural and agricultural region that offered them no pool of skilled labor. Suitable quality construction materials were often scarce, particularly the stone, lime, and cement required for masonry works. Demands for lime and cement for the canal resulted in the establishment of enduring businesses for the production of these commodities along its line. A combined shortage of money and readily available quality stone in the canal's upper reaches eventually necessitated modifying how the locks were constructed. Chamber walls of these 13 locks, known as composite locks, were made of rubble and undressed stone covered with double layers of treated planks. (One lock originally in the plan was unneeded and dropped as an economy measure. Omission of this projected Lock 65 accounts for the odd numbering: Lock 62, Lock 63⅓, Lock 64⅔, Lock 66.)

The canal set up its own sawmill operation on the Virginia side of Great Falls to mill planks and locust beams for constructing the lock gates. Along the line, similar operations were eventually established as needed. Tools were primitive: picks, shovels, wheelbarrows, and wagons and scoops drawn by draft animals. Basically, these were the same tools that had been used to build canals in Europe for the past 200 years or more. Land costs mushroomed as owners held out for higher and higher payments and courts awarded them. Charles Carroll, who had broken ground for the B&O Railroad on the same day that President Adams broke ground for the canal, owned a large estate over which the canal had to pass. A powerful Marylander, Carroll held out to the bitter end in legal machinations to frustrate the canal's push westward. Protracted court battles with the railroad over a right-of-way through the river narrows at Point of Rocks, Maryland, would cost the canal project precious time and money and devastate investor confidence.

After examining 462 proposals submitted by some 100 contractors, the board let contracts in late 1828 for 34 sections between Little Falls and Seneca Creek. Most of the successful bidders had prior experience in the construction of canals in New York, Pennsylvania, Ohio, Connecticut, and Canada: 18 of the contracts, worth $160,000 of the total $218,000 let, were secured by New York and Pennsylvania contractors.

Wright was hired as chief engineer on June 23, 1828, less than two weeks before the groundbreaking. On June 26, canal president Charles F. Mercer informed the canal board that notice had been served upon him on June 24 "of an injunction granted by Theodore Bland, Chancellor of the State of Maryland, at the suit of the Baltimore and Ohio Railroad Company." The injunction prevented the construction of the canal above Point of Rocks. Before either canal or railroad had even broken ground, the race was on and the lines of battle were drawn. The dispute would halt work at that point for nearly four years. It would also delay, for four years, the opening of the entire canal section from above the Seneca feeder dam to Harpers Ferry. There the next feeder dam was required to inject Potomac water into the canal system. It took more than two years just to open the first section of 17 miles from Little Falls to Seneca. The first boat of record made the run on October 1, 1830.

Over level terrain in an uninhabited landscape the task of canal building would have been relatively simple. Just hire enough common laborers to dig a trench across the plain and then make it watertight. No plain lay in wait for the C&O Canal's builders, however. They had to overcome a 605-foot change in elevation over the 184.5 miles between tidewater at the canal's terminus in Georgetown and Cumberland at the base of the Allegheny Mountains. Confronting a hill the canal engineer had three choices: build the canal around the hill; build the canal up one side of the hill and down the other; or go through the hill, either by cutting or tunneling. Canals also had to negotiate artificial obstacles such as roads. Roads must either pass under the canal or be carried over it. Natural obstacles such as rivers and streams posed like problems. Some 160 functioning culverts testify to the myriad of streams, drainages, or roads that passed under the canal. Eleven aqueducts carried the canal itself over rivers and streams that were too big for culverts to handle. All such negotiations of terrain and obstacles had to be accomplished by level sections of water—hence the term "flatwater route." In effect, the C&O Canal is a linear succession of level ponds of varying lengths built step-like in tiers across the landscape.

Locks are most often used to overcome changes in the level of the ground through which the canal must pass. A lock is a chamber with watertight gates at both ends. Sluices in the lock gates themselves can regulate the flow of water into and out of the chamber. Locks can be filled with or emptied of their water in about 10 minutes, raising or lowering the canal boat to the next level. Boats are thereby stepped up or down between canal levels. The C&O Canal used 74 lift locks to step boats up from Georgetown to Cumberland. Twelve river feeder locks and guard locks regulated the flow of Potomac River water into and out of the canal's water system or passed boats between the canal and the river. Guard locks also gave protection to the canal and its structures in periods of high water. With the introduction of culverts, waste weirs, aqueducts, bridges, locks, and lock gates into the canal construction scenario, masons, stonecutters, carpenters, and blacksmiths had to be incorporated into the work force along with diggers.

By closely following the Potomac River watercourse, the C&O Canal did not have to cross wide, steep valleys; such terrain challenges account for some of the magnificent, high aqueducts that grace European canals. C&O Canal aqueducts were required only to carry the canal across major tributary streams just above their mouths. In three places where the Potomac has cut only the narrowest of passages through the mountains or hills, there was not enough space to place the canal. Such situations gave rise to two slackwater navigations and the Paw Paw Tunnel. At slackwater navigations, boatmen had to take their boats out of the quiet canal and into the Potomac

Today one of the Potomac's finest wild areas, the Paw Paw Bends held a different surprise for canal builders. Tortuous river meanders here would require 6 miles of canal to negotiate a mile's westward progress. The canal company chose to tunnel through a mountain for 3,118 feet to save the extra 5 miles. Resistant rock and money and labor problems strung out the tunnel project from 1836 to 1848. This helped delay the canal's completion to Cumberland until 1850.

River for a distance before locking back in where the canal continued upstream or downstream. Construction alternatives—cutting or tunneling through rock ridges running right down to the river's edge—were impractical. Navigating a powerful river in a heavily laden, flatbottomed boat with no keel proved harrowing for many a boatman. Remarkably few cargoes and boats were lost in these slackwater navigations, however. At the Paw Paw Bends area between Hancock and Cumberland the canal's engineers opted to tunnel 3,118 feet through such a ridge rather than to follow tortuous river meanders that would entail some 6 additional miles of canal construction but gain less than a mile of westward progress. The tunnel would prove a major obstacle to completing the canal in a timely fashion.

Canal board members realized almost from the outset that sufficient laborers—common and skilled—for their giant task were not locally available. However, they could hardly have envisioned the magnitude of labor problems that would ensue and, in one instance, even necessitate intervention by federal troops. Late in 1828, the canal board decided to advertise for laborers in Europe. In the first half of 1829 the canal company hired an agent in Great Britain to secure common laborers to work on the canal, negotiated for workers from the British Isles through the American consul at Liverpool, and decided to engage the services of 300 stonecutters and masons from Europe who had participated in numerous canal projects. The company further decided to make loans to its contractors that would enable them to transport additional stonecutters and masons from other parts of the United States.

Many canal laborers came over on indenture agreements that afforded them passage to the United States in return for a specified number of years' labor on the canal. For its part the canal company additionally offered certain wages and agreed to provide daily allotments of meat and alcoholic beverages. However, both the company and the workers felt, time and again, that the other party had not lived up to the agreement. Movements to organize labor had barely begun in the Nation's industrial centers at this time and were nonexistent in the agricultural Potomac Valley. Hence, no formal mechanism existed either for negotiations or the resolution of disputes.

Preceding pages: *Impressive and enduring aqueducts testify to the canal's engineering finesse. The 3-span Conococheague Aqueduct carried the canal across Conococheague Creek at Williamsport, Md. Eleven aqueducts graced the canal's length. Perhaps the most beautiful is the 7-span Monocacy Aqueduct across the Monocacy River. Attempts by Confederate troops to blow it up during the Civil War were foiled by its stout masonry.*

Alcohol provisions of the indenture agreements repeatedly fueled difficulties. Workers felt that the company cheated them regarding the promises of alcohol, and the company asserted that the consumption of alcohol was causing many of the problems of breached agreements and consequent delays in construction progress.

Eventually, many indentured workers abandoned their agreements and fled the canal project to Baltimore. To the canal company's great consternation, many of these workers promptly secured jobs on the B&O Railroad project. Furthermore, Baltimore courts, surely under the influence of that city's keen interest in the competing railroad project, made little or no effort to secure prosecution of workers on the basis of indenture agreements with the canal.

Disputes among laboring factions were also a major problem. Conflicts frequently occurred between groups of laborers from different ethnic or national backgrounds. Conflicts also developed between groups of workers from different sections of Ireland.

When construction activity was at its peak on the C&O line, however, the scene must have been a wondrous, dizzy stir of activity. Hundreds of workers wielded picks and axes, worked stump pullers, followed horse-drawn plows and scrapers, filled wheelbarrows by the shovelful, carpentered, mixed lime for mortar, and prepared, moved, and placed stone for locks and lockhouses, culverts, waste weirs, aqueducts, and other canal structures.

In 1832, the canal company at last won court ratification of its right-of-way at Point of Rocks and approval to proceed with construction above that site. Looking toward its first full summer of unrestricted construction potential, the company nevertheless saw significant problems looming ahead: it was running out of both time and money. In 1833, the five years that the canal company charter allowed for building the first 100 miles would expire. Also, the company's immediate financial resources were approaching exhaustion—indeed, it suffered its first bankruptcy in 1832. Another unforeseen disaster befell the canal line in August 1832 in the form of Asiatic cholera. It struck first near Harpers Ferry and moved gradually westward to Williamsport. Fear spread among canal workers and valley residents. Many laborers died; others fled in panic. By early winter, when the epidemic began to subside, the waterway's westward progress had almost halted.

Of all the geological surprises to confront the canal engineers and construction crews, none provoked such frustrations as the tunnel through a mountain at the Potomac's Paw Paw Bends, an area now considered one of the Potomac's finest wild areas. The alternatives to a tunnel were another slackwater navigation, crossing the river with the canal, or pushing it through difficult terrain for some 6 miles. The tunnel route could be located above the level of recurring floods. Also, it would require just one mile of construction, thereby eliminating 5 miles of canal and towpath construction and reducing canal boat travel time. Naked stratifications of rock here would make the canal prism expensive to excavate and difficult to protect from flood damage. These facts, coupled with optimistic engineering reports, caused the canal board to build the tunnel. The result would be the canal's major feature, a magnificent engineering feat, but the projected two-year construction schedule would stretch to 12 years and the project come in at 300 percent over budget. Crews set to work in June 1836, and the tunnel was not completed until 1848. Not until 1850 could boats pass the canal's complete length from Cumberland to Georgetown.

The canal's grand opening in 1850 occasioned flowery speeches in Georgetown and Cumberland, and the canal company cherished high hopes for turning ready profits. Again, there was even talk of pushing on to Pittsburgh and the Ohio River, but this was never to be. The canal's engineering and construction achievements, with one exception, were all now behind it. The exception was the incline plane to be built above Georgetown in the 1870s, when for a time the canal prospered. This engineering marvel, recognized at the 1878 Paris Exposition, carried boats from the canal down to the Potomac River to alleviate traffic jams among the more than 500 boats operating on the canal in those years. Despite this engineering afterthought, however, the great national project, this heir to George Washington's dream, had been realized upon its completion. The widest, deepest, and sixth longest canal in the Nation had been pushed from tidewater to the Cumberland coalfields at the foot of the Allegheny Mountains.

From Tidal Water to the Allegheny Mountains

By the 19th century, Americans were tapping the natural resources of the Ohio Valley and the Allegheny highlands. Mid-Atlantic tidewater ports could distribute the goods, but ports and resources were separated by a formidable mountain barrier. The Potomac River cut through the mountains and emptied into the Chesapeake Bay, but its upper reaches provided unreliable navigation. It did, however, have level terraces—old floodplains—along which canals could be dug. With its tributaries, the river drained over 10,000 square miles of land (right) and could provide a steady supply of water to a canal. In fact, the drainage system was so large that during heavy rains the narrow river channel often could not contain the increased flow, which would ultimately prove disastrous to the canal. The changing landscape through which the river passes posed a variety of other problems for the builders. On the river's broad floodplain between White's Ferry and Seneca, construction was relatively easy. But for much of its length the river flowed through a narrow, steep-walled valley, especially in the gaps at Harpers Ferry and Point of Rocks, and workers had to blast out rock to create a ledge for the canal. At Great Falls and Mather Gorge, the canal ran along a cliff at a dizzying height above the river.

Natural Provinces

In its course from mountains to tidewater, the ancient Potomac travels through six physiographic provinces. As it leaves the rugged Allegheny Plateau it enters the Ridge and Valley province of folded sandstone ridges and valleys formed by rivers cutting through soft limestone. The Shenandoah Valley is part of the Great Valley that runs from Alabama to Pennsylvania. The easternmost ridges are those in the Blue Ridge province, where great gaps were created by simultaneous uplift and erosion. From here the river flows through the rolling Piedmont province until it reaches the Coastal Plain province and tidewater below Little Falls.

ALLEGHENY PLATEAU PROVINCE

Wills Creek

Cumberland

Har

Potomac River

North Branch

Paw Paw Tunnel

RIDGE AND VALLEY PROVINCE

South Branch

SHENANDOA VALLE

APPALACHIAN MOUNTAINS

BLUE RIDGE

The Landscape's Profile

It is easier for us to appreciate the scope of the canal builders' achievement when the physical obstacles are simplified and shown in profile (below). They had to reduce this widely varying terrain, as it fell some 605 feet, to a series of precise, vertical steps. The task required 74 locks, each of which dropped the boats an average of 8 feet. Because the land is sometimes level and sometimes falls off sharply, the distance between the locks varies widely: 9.5 miles separate locks 40 and 41 near Williamsport, while the six locks at Great Falls span less than a mile. Whatever the distance, the canal had

Cumberland

Paw Paw Tunnel

Hancock

Four Locks

Williamsport

500ft

300ft

100ft

The Potomac drainage basin

The Potomac River Valley

CUMBERLAND VALLEY
Four Locks
Williamsport
BLUE RIDGE PROVINCE
GREAT VALLEY PROVINCE
Shenandoah River
Brunswick
Harpers Ferry
Point of Rocks
White's Ferry
Potomac River
Seneca
Great Falls
Seven Locks
Georgetown
Washington, D.C.
Alexandria
PIEDMONT PROVINCE
MARYLAND
Patuxent River
VIRGINIA
COASTAL PLAIN PROVINCE
CHESAPEAKE BAY
POTOMAC RIVER

to be absolutely level between the locks. Water in the canal did not flow downward like a river. Rather, it was impounded in levels and then released, 74 times, on its descent to tidewater.

A survey ordered by the canal company in 1889 made precise topographical charts of the terrain. Steps indicate lift locks. The survey was kept current until the U.S. Government bought the canal in 1938.

Harpers Ferry

| 0 | 5 | 10 Kilometers |
| 0 | 5 | 10 Miles |

Great Falls

Georgetown

Seven Locks

Building the Canal

It was all done with hand tools and horse power. Construction did not simply begin at one end and progress steadily to the other end, leaving a finished canal in its wake. The job was let to dozens of contractors in ½-mile sections, and, for the most part, they worked simultaneously. The activities shown here would not have been performed concurrently or so close together. In the distance, the tunnel is being dug **1**. Blasting was often necessary to clear a path for the canal. After trees were cut or broken **2**, stumps were pulled with huge, horse-powered winches **3**. Root-cutting plows **4** scraped the surface in preparation for the digging **5**, berm-building **6**, and puddling with waterproof clay **7**. With cut stone **8**, pre-built lock gates **9**, and iron hardware shipped to the site, workers constructed aqueducts **10**, feeder dams **11**, guard locks **12**, culverts **13**, retaining walls **14**, lift locks and flumes **15**, waste weirs **16**, and stop locks **17**.

Instead of following the slope of the land, a canal periodically takes a vertical step between levels of flat water. This is accomplished at a series of locks, which on the C&O averaged a drop of 8 feet. The locks' hand-operated mitre gates were simple, virtually unchanged from Leonardo da Vinci's original 1485 design (right). The operation, though, demanded experience and close attention. As a boatman approached a lock, he would sound his horn a half to a quarter mile away, alerting the lockkeeper. Entering the lock was the most demanding part of canalling. The boat fit the lock with only 3 inches to spare on both sides, and if the helmsman allowed a loaded boat to hit the lock walls, he could damage or even sink the boat. Such a blow could also damage the masonry. Once in the lock, the 93-foot boat—only 7 feet shorter than the lock—had to have enough momentum to go all the way in, but had to be stopped before it crashed into the gate at the other end. A crew member jumped ashore and turned a heavy rope around the snubbing post to brake the boat. This was an art in itself: too tight and the momentum of the boat would break the post. Now the locking-through operation could begin. One crew set a record of 3 minutes, but 8 to 10 minutes was a good time.

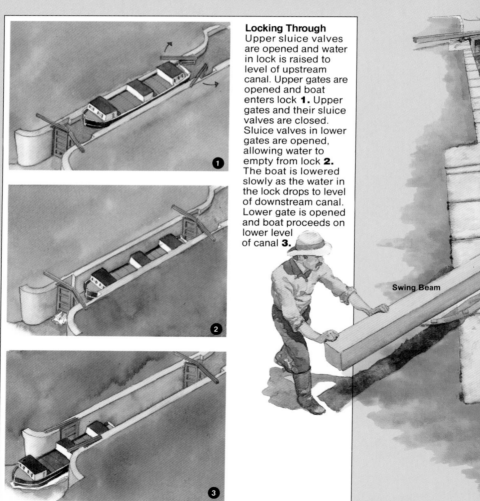

Locking Through
Upper sluice valves are opened and water in lock is raised to level of upstream canal. Upper gates are opened and boat enters lock **1.** Upper gates and their sluice valves are closed. Sluice valves in lower gates are opened, allowing water to empty from lock **2.** The boat is lowered slowly as the water in the lock drops to level of downstream canal. Lower gate is opened and boat proceeds on lower level of canal **3.**

Swing Beam

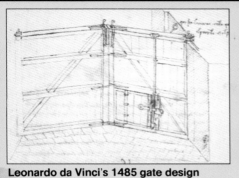
Leonardo da Vinci's 1485 gate design

Canal boat exiting a lock

Lock Key

Sluice Valve

Mitre Sill

Engineering Achievements

The grand scale of the canal project can over-shadow the high level of engineering represented by the individual structures. Without today's sophisticated tools and equipment, the engineers created enduring structures of strength and beauty. Detailed general plans were drawn for the series of aqueducts, dams, and culverts. But the need to adapt the structures to available materials and local conditions—often in water or on rugged terrain—created an interesting variety of sizes and designs. Their fine masonry work and graceful lines are reminders of an age when the scale was human and standards of craft were high.

More than 150 stone **culverts** made up the largest engineering project on the Canal.

Some on the upper canal were built of wood and brick.

The bed of the canal was called the **"prism"** because the top was wider than the bottom. The specified dimensions—60 feet wide at a water level of 6 feet and 48 feet at the bottom—were followed below Harpers Ferry, but the prism was generally smaller on the upper canal. The prism was the largest of U.S. canals, leaving enough water at the sides of the boats to allow unimpeded movement—essentially like open-water navigation.

Most dramatic and beautiful of the structures were the 11 **aqueducts.** Stone-cutting and laying had to be precise so the bed, or "trunk," would not leak.

Most of the seven river **dams** that watered the canal were built of heavy timber cribs anchored to the river bed and filled with quarried stone and rubble.

The 3,118-foot **Paw Paw Tunnel** (below), considered the greatest single engineering achievement on the canal, took 12 years to build.

37

The Georgetown Incline Plane

To compete with the expanding railroads, the C&O Canal had to eliminate inefficiencies, the worst being the long backups at Georgetown. The solution was an incline plane, completed in 1876, to transfer boats from the canal to the Potomac River above Georgetown. A 112-foot caisson on angled wheel trucks was secured to the upper lock and filled with water to the canal level. The boat moved into the caisson, the gates were closed, and the caisson was lowered down the 4½° slope. With the water volume adjusted so water, boat, and caisson were balanced by the counterweights, the machinery had only to overcome friction to lower the caisson. At the bottom, when the water level in the caisson equaled that of the river, the gates were opened and the boat passed into the river. Despite problems caused by the great loads on the machinery and rails, the incline was used until it was destroyed by the flood of 1889.

Canal

Incline Entrance Lock

Winding Pulleys

Caisson and Floating Canal Boat

Counterweights

Turbine Tailrace

Caisson

Pawl-and-Ratchet Brakes

Canal boatmen spent a fifth of the time it took to complete a trip waiting their turn to unload at the Georgetown terminus. While they waited they were charged exorbitant fees by wharf owners. The incline plane let them transfer from the canal to the Potomac River in half the time it took to use the Rock Creek outlet.

The **incline plane** was the most sophisticated piece of engineering on the canal. The drawing shows how water was drawn off the canal to power the turbine. It turned massive winding pulleys that carried the steel cables attached to the caisson and counterweights. In Europe, where canals had remained an important means of transport, the C&O incline was discussed in technical journals of the period. The structure was among those selected to represent American engineering achievements at the Paris Exposition of 1878.

Turbine Headrace

Incline Entrance Lock

Winding Pulleys

Water Turbine

Steel Cables

The massive weights of the **loaded caisson** (360-400 tons), and counterweights (200 tons each), made failure of the machinery potentially disastrous. Both the friction brakes and a pawl-and-ratchet system failed in 1877 when masonry supporting the cable pulleys gave way. The caisson and counterweights ran out of control, killing three men. After that, the boats were lowered in dry caissons to reduce the weight.

Potomac River

The Canal at Work

In preparing for a journey down the 185-mile length of the C&O Canal, the boatman needed to obtain feed and provisions for his family and mules. Hay and feed for the mules were purchased at various establishments across from the coal-loading wharves at the basin in Cumberland. The usual staples for a trip consisted of flour, sugar, coffee, smoked meat, and dry salt belly. Since the sale of liquor was outlawed along the canal, alcoholic beverages also were purchased at the stores at the canal basin or at the numerous saloons that operated in Shantytown around and behind the Cumberland boatyards. Saloons went by such names as Old Aunt Susan Jones' Rising Sun Saloon and Mis' Palmer's Red Tin Shanty. If the captain's family was not large enough to provide the needed help on the boat, he made arrangements to hire a deck hand or two, sometimes for a single trip and sometimes for the season.

When preparations were made, the captain backed his boat up to the coal chutes at the loading basin. The coal was dumped out of the railroad cars on a trestle over the chutes and passed down the chutes into the holds of the canal boat. After having received a way bill from the canal company collector, the boat commenced its run down the canal.

A normal trip to Georgetown took about four or five 18-hour days. A roundtrip, according to some records, could be made in 7 days. Today, traffic permitting, the Cumberland-to-Georgetown trip can take less than 3 hours by car. At ten minutes locking-through time per each of 74 lift locks, 12½ hours were consumed just in the locks. The canal offered a 2½ m.p.h. current, but its speed limit was set at 4 m.p.h. to protect the banks from erosion. In the canal's 9-month operating period, captains usually made 25 trips per year. Although some boats ran all night, most tied up in groups of six or seven between 10 p.m. and 4 a.m.

U.S. Army quartermaster records during the Civil

War reveal the names of many canal boats that carried coal for the government during that conflict. Many were simply named for individuals, but more colorful monikers were not uncommon. *Liberty, Prince Rupert, Independence, Odd Fellow, Emperor, Union, Mt. Savage,* and *Hard Times* were among these. Boats might also be multi-colored, carefully decorated, and highly individualistic. However, at the time of the canal's final closing in 1924, all the canal boats were owned by the Canal Towage Company and simply bore numbers and uniform paint jobs.

The usual schedule both for the mules and the crew was six hours of work and six hours of rest. Work shifts were called "tricks." Members of the captain's family generally slept in the rear, or stern, compartment (see boat illustration on pages 56 and 57) if there was room. This 12- by 12½-foot cabin was entered by a short stairs and contained a galley, with dining table and cupboards, and a stateroom. Hired hands or the older members of large families slept in the hay house, which had bunks on one side and feed on the other. Although this may sound like close quarters, many canallers described their life more as lonely than as crowded.

Some boatmen took Sunday off to attend church services in the small towns along the canal, but most of the canallers, who generally appeared to be an irreverent and irreligious lot, boated seven days a week if loads were available. Eventually, canallers became the target of missionary work and, just before the canal closed for good, the U.S. Department of Labor conducted a study of the lot of canal boat children.

Most everything that was needed by canallers in the way of groceries or feed could be purchased along the canal. Many stores, in numbers that today's hikers and bicyclists would envy, catered to the needs of the boatmen both at many of the locks and in the villages in the vicinity of the canal. Records of at

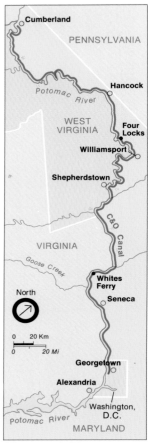

Many canal-side towns prospered as ports of call when trade began on the canal. Today's Georgetown—where the canal is watered—and Williamsport best retain their canal flavors. Williamsport linked nearby Hagerstown and the productive Cumberland Valley with the coastal trade via Georgetown and Alexandria. Many boat captains had their winter homes in Williamsport.

least 27 stores right along the canal have been found. In addition, most lockkeepers raised milk cows, chickens, and vegetables. The surplus of these was sold to the canallers. Some boatmen, however, carried chickens and one or two pigs on their boats to reduce expenses and supplemented their diet with fish and turtles from the canal.

Duties of the women on the canal boats included cooking, child-rearing, cleaning, washing, and sewing. Women often helped steer the boats and feed the mules. They cooked on the cabin stove, which was usually fueled with burned corn cobs from the stable. Cobs provided hot, quick fires for the small cabin space. Some of the boats had more modern stoves, known as Star Light coal burners, made with coke tin by a Cumberland firm. Two of the most popular dishes among the boatmen were soup made from turtles caught in the canal, and blackberry pie made from berries growing wild along the towpath.

Canal boat women had their babies on the boats; if possible the boat would stop at a town where the services of a midwife could be obtained. Then the journey was resumed the next day, with the man handling most of the cooking chores unless he had older children. Women often washed clothes and bathed children at the side of the canal in the moonlight after the boat had tied up for the night. They frequently sewed or mended clothes and awnings for the boat leaning against the "stick" that guided the boat's rudder. If a captain died, his widow often ran the boat herself.

To prevent falls into the canal, the youngest children were buckled into a leather or rope harness and tied fast with a line—or chained—to the ring bolt in the cabin roof. By the age of six, most children were put to work driving the mules. Most captains got their start on the canal as children, walking beside the mules on the towpath, holding a four-strand, plaited whip. The children were permitted frequently to ride the lead mule to protect their feet and to prevent them from tiring. The canallers' children generally had little opportunity to go to school, except during the winter months when the canal froze up and their families lived in town. Extended occupational isolation meant that the canal people tended to cohere over the years, intermarrying and creating a subculture. A captain who owned his canal boat was no gypsy, however. In 1859, for example, canal boats cost $1,200 to $1,500, sums that might approach the equivalence of $100,000 in today's currency. Most captains also owned a home as well.

When a boat approached a lock, the steersman got out his boat horn, generally a tin bugle, and blew the three notes of "Red Rover." Supposedly the boathorn was saying "Lock Ready! Lock Ready! Lock Ready!" If no horn was available, the steersman or driver, whoever had the loudest voice, would yell: "Yea-a-a-a-a-a lock!" or "Hey-y-y-y-y-y Lock!" Some boatmen used conch shells to announce their approach. During the day, the lockkeeper often saw the boat before he heard the call, but at night he had to be awakened.

Locking-through was a procedure made delicate by the fit of boat to lock. Locks were the limiting factor in boat size, and boat size was the limiting factor in profit. Boats eventually were standardized to fit snugly into the locks, with just inches to spare on the sides and no room to spare at the ends. The rudder, in fact, had to be laid against the stern so that lock gates could be closed. Stout snubbing posts and a heavy line to the boat were used to brake and to stabilize the canal boat inside the lock. Otherwise, the lock's churning water tended to throw the boat against the delicate masonry walls or the lock's far gate. Steering was an art—guiding this keelless, cumbersome, oak-bottomed freight boat off the levels into such confined space. It would be touchier than trying to submerge a tight-fitting tabletop in a full bathtub without bumping its sides.

The mules, many of which came from Kentucky, were broken in by hitching them to logs. New mules, called "greenies," often sat down and refused to move. This problem was solved by hitching several trained mules to the "sitdowner" and dragging it along until standing up was more comfortable than sitting down. Mules were hard on their shoes, so they were reshod on an average of once a month.

Mules were generally purchased when they were 2½ years old. As a rule, they lasted some 15 years before they became too old and infirm to be of value. Each boatman kept two teams of two or three mules each with his boat. Good experienced mules often did not require a driver. They slacked off automatically when a boatman was snubbing a boat into a

CANAL Packet Boat GEO. WASHINGTON.
The Packet Boat George Washington will commence her daily trips to Crommelin and Seneca tomorrow morning, leaving the temporary lock above Georgetown at ½ past 7 o'clock, to return the same evening. The proprietors will spare no effort on their part to render satisfaction to all who patronize their boat. They are provided with good teams, and every arrangement is made in their boat and bar for the comfort of the public.

Parties wishing to make an excursion to either of the above places, by giving short notice, will be accommodated in best style. Those who have not already enjoyed the delight, which the scenery of the contiguous country, and the great work itself, (the Chesapeake and Ohio Canal) afford, will now have the opportunity of gratifying themselves.

Fare to Crommelin   37½ cents.
"   to Seneca   50 cents.
Same returning.

P. S. In a few days the proprietors hope to get their Boat into Georgetown, when they will, until further notice, leave the Market House, at the hour above named, and return to the same spot.
SAMUEL CUNNINGHAM,
THOS. NOWLAN.
Georgetown, July 12—tf

Packet boats carried passengers on the canal in its early days, as this handbill suggests. This hoped-for enterprise never met canal company expectations. Excursion boats later ran from Georgetown to Great Falls, but the C&O did not become a passenger route as had the Erie Canal. "Crommelin" here refers to the Great Falls area.

Chartered in March 1825, the Chesapeake and Ohio Canal Company broke ground on July 4, 1828. The company, whose seal is shown above, enjoyed as investors the City of Washington, Georgetown, Alexandria, the State of Maryland, and Shepherdstown, Va., now W. Va. Some private citizens also invested. Virginia withdrew when it learned the entire route would follow the Maryland side of the Potomac River.

lock, and once through a lock they took off on the cue of the steersman's whistle. If a boatman wished to change his teams, the mules reacted to verbal commands. Mules could shy, however, when snakes crossed—or simply lay in—the towpath, which was a frequent occurrence.

Generally, the mules were changed while the boat was passing through a lock—a feat that required fast work. A short fallboard, much like a cleated gangplank, was thrown over the side of the boat when the water in the lock chamber was at its highest level, and a fresh team from the stable in the bow was herded out quickly. Handling mule teams at times proved overburdening for children, especially when boats had to pass each other on the canal. A 12-foot-wide towpath could hardly be called two-laned for teams of mules, particularly if any of the individuals were inexperienced. In fact, on the towpath, mule teams probably got to know each other more intimately than canal boat captains knew their peers. In the canal's heyday, 10 to 11 mules per mile worked the towpath.

Rights-of-way were regulated, in that all craft had to pass on the right. Loaded boats, those going downstream, had the right-of-way over light boats. Additionally, all boats had precedence over rafts, packet boats over freight boats, and mail packets over all. (In the canal's later years, when passenger service was nil, loaded boats also gained the right-of-way over packets.) When boats were to pass, one mule team had to stop and let its towline go slack to lie in the water and on the towpath so that the passing team could cross it. This also meant lines had to sink, so the canal boat could cross as well. Lines would only sink if wet, so mule drivers had to make sure they stayed wet, or else get them wet in anticipation of being passed if their boat lacked the right-of-way in a developing encounter. With clouds of horseflies, free-ranging hogs, and multitudinous snakes on the towpath, the passing of boats saddled the mule driver with great responsibility.

A good dog was a great help with the mules and was sometimes used to drive them. One captain's bull dog could swim across the canal basin at Cumberland with a towline around his neck—a great help when the mules and boats were separated on opposite sides of the basin.

passing of the distinctive C&O Canal
ture was symbolized by the presence of
last surviving canal mule, Mutt, at a 1939
emony dedicating the canal as a recrea-
nal waterway. It was a way of life that
dured for almost a century, but the photo-
aphic record covers only the last few dec-
es. This was the period during which the
allers lost their independence. The Ca-
Towage Co. controlled all cargo con-
cts, standardized the boats, and replaced
eir names with numbers. But daily life
ng the canal changed little, and the
otographs capture the flavor of canal
ciety.

milies such as the father and son taking
. 32 toward a lock continued to make up
e core of the crews. Their life on the boats
s a quiet routine of work and domestic
ores, punctuated with moments of relaxa-
n and play—and, as boatmen were often a
ugh and rowdy lot, fights with lockkeepers.
e cargo, being the livelihood of the family,
ok precedence over everything. It left
tle living room on the boat, and most of the
mily's 18-hour day was devoted to moving
e load down the canal. Only the youngest
ildren were exempt from work and could
ile away their days playing on the cabin
of. Their range was limited, however, by
e tethers that kept them from falling into
e canal. Despite the often fetid state of the
nal water, it was hard to keep the older
ildren out of it. But boys and girls by this
ge had regular duties to perform. They were
sponsible for the all-important mules,
nding them on board and driving them on
e canal path. While driving the mules was
sually routine, the driver had to be able to
andle them when they were spooked by a
nake across their path or the whistle of a
earby locomotive.

a few years young people would be given
e ultimate responsibility on a canal boat—
teering. The hours on the quiet stretches
etween locks could be tedious, but en-
ounters with other boats and locking-
hrough furnished the opportunity for all-
oo-brief exchanges with other canallers.
Blacks worked as deckhands on boats from
he earliest years, but until the post-Civil
War era, were banned from owning boats.
During the canal's heyday in the 1870s, four
lacks were listed as Captains. In the final

Father and son approach lock 44

THE WAS

Last C. & O. Canal Mule Dies

Mut, last of
a numberless
legion of
mules that
pulled barges
through the
locks and
levels of the
Chesapeake
& Potomac
Canal, died
Wednesday.
Mutt is
shown with
Harry Mur-
ray, a former
canal em-
ploye on Feb-
ruary 22,
1939 at the
dedication of
the canal in
Georgetown
as a recrea-
tional water-
way

Mules were part of the fabric of canal life

Canal boat children, c. 1910

Off-loading coal at Williamsport

Young mule driver

Taking a turn at the tiller, c. 1910

One of the few black canal boat captains

Raymond Riley was born in the lockhouse at Riley's Lock, tended by his father, John, from 1892 to 1924 when the canal closed down. Both John Riley and his father, William, who came over from Ireland at age 16, worked at the Seneca Stone Cutting Mill. The quarry and mill produced the beautiful Seneca Red Sandstone used on the canal and to build the "castle" at the Smithsonian Institution in Washington, D.C.

When the canal got icy, a canal company scow, loaded with pig iron, started up the waterway from Georgetown to serve as an icebreaker. Homeward-bound boats, all light and heading for winter quarters, formed a procession behind the ice breaker. As many as 40 mules from the boats in the procession would be hooked to the ice breaker's towline. The animals would haul the boat up on the ice and her weight would break a channel through which the boats would pass. The entire convoy would help pump water out of a boat if the ice broke a hole in it. The members of the procession also would hack at the ice with their axes if necessary. If a boat was frozen solid, the captain and crew simply closed it up and rode the mules home.

Boatmen tied up their boats as close to home as possible. In the 1850s, most boatmen kept a home where they spent the winter months—in Cumberland, Georgetown, Williamsport, Alexandria, Washington, Hancock, Shepherdstown, or Antietam (Sharpsburg). In 1873-74, the majority hailed from Cumberland, Williamsport, Sharpsburg, Bakersville, and Hancock. The change reflects the growing dependence of the canal on the coal trade that originated in Cumberland. Some canallers simply lived aboard their tied-up boats over the winter.

From the first navigation on the canal, in 1830, the canal's board of directors reserved much authority for themselves that should have fallen to section superintendents. As a result, lockkeepers assumed an exaggerated importance to the welfare of the canal's operation as superintendents foundered for their lack of line authority. Wages for lockkeepers were originally set before the canal's first section was watered. Annual wages were not to exceed $150 for a single lock, $200 for two locks, and $250 for three locks. As the canal set to open above Little Falls, however, the company already felt a financial crunch and, when the first lockkeepers were actually hired, wages were set below those maximums, at $50 to $200.

In place of the higher pay, lockkeepers were to be allowed to use at least one acre of company land for gardening. Produce they ate would help compensate for lower pay; excess produce they sold would supplement it. Each lockkeeper also was soon supplied with tools to be used to preserve and repair the portion of the canal under his care. Responsibilities for inspecting the section under his care came with the tools. Level walkers, as they were called, were hired to inspect, on a regular, continuing basis, specified sections of the canal. Heading off problems that could lead to breaches in the canal prism was a priority.

By 1884, the canal was administratively divided into two districts for payroll purposes. Records for that year show that each division had a superintendent, collector, and clerk. The Georgetown end also had a harbormaster, assistants to the collector and superintendent, 42 lockkeepers, a telephone superintendent, chief engineer and assistant engineer for the Georgetown Incline (see illustration on pages 38 and 39), 4 incline helpers, 3 boss carpenters, 8 carpenters, smith, caulker, laborers, level walkers, masons, cooks, boss of dredge, dredging engineer, dipper tender, and firemen. Division 2 had 35 lockkeepers, a gauger, steam packet operator, and 5 mud machine laborers. The harbormaster's counterpart at Cumberland was the (boat) basin clerk. At the basin there were also watchman, trimmers, dumpers, driver, and hostler positions. Payroll records for April 1884 show 328 salaried and wage-earning employees on the canal drawing a total of $12,308.51 that month, with some deductions for room and board. That represented a healthy boost to local economies of that time.

For boatmen journeying down the canal, it was the lockkeeper, not the section superintendents or company directors, who represented the canal company, both symbolically and in fact. Here was someone for the canaller alternately to fight or fraternize with at 74 locks per one-way trip. Here also was a source of fresh garden produce and maybe a loaf of fresh-baked bread for the boatman. Many a songfest took place in the cramped shelter of the lockkeepers' shanties on rainy or cold nights. Many a wistful, romantic gaze, passed between the offspring of the canallers and those of the lockkeeper who gazed on the slowly passing boats. For their own part the lockkeepers worked hard—and long. If a boatman traveled round the clock, the lockkeepers had to be prepared to lock him through round the clock. Accordingly, many slept, not in the house with their families, but in the shanty right by the lock. There they listened for the boatman's horn, or for his cry of "Hey-y-y-y-y-y Lock!" that signaled that the C&O Canal was, whatever the hour, hard at work.

Evelyn Pryor Liston spent her first day on a canal boat at age 11 or 12—and didn't like it one bit. She got homesick leaving the family place in Williamsport. She and her slightly older sister kept house on their father's boat; Harry Pryor didn't like cooking or washing dishes. Later Evelyn crewed with a younger sister and sometimes would steer the boat when it wasn't loaded. Her father could tend to the mules then. After high school and a job, Evelyn went back on her father's boat for the last year the canal was open.

Serving the Potomac Valley

Pushing westward from thriving tidewater ports near the Nation's Capital and at Baltimore, the C&O Canal and the B&O Railroad brought innumerable benefits to the predominantly agricultural Potomac Valley. Keenly competitive freight rates proved a boon to regional industries, mining, and agriculture. The canal itself spurred development of new industries. Although some benefits the canal brought were short-lived, others persisted through its operating years. Several would leave lasting imprints on life in the Potomac River Basin.

By July 4, 1828, when construction officially began for both canal and railroad, George Washington's dream of opening the Allegheny Mountains region and the Ohio Valley was yet to be realized in the mid-Atlantic states. The Erie Canal was starting to provide a major conduit for settlement of western lands, but the wealth of the Ohio country that had captured Washington's imagination increasingly flowed to tidewater at New York City instead of down the Potomac River past the Nation's Capital and Mount Vernon to the sea.

First to benefit from the canal's push west were landowners—and almost as quickly their lawyers—in its right-of-way. Land acquisition costs projected at $1,000 per mile quickly jumped to $2,290 per mile. Court-awarded settlements soon boosted land costs 2½ to 25 times higher than initial company projections. Part of the problem lay with railroad competition. Charles Carroll of Carrollton, who held a major interest in the railroad, owned a 10,000-acre Frederick County estate in the canal right-of-way, and he brushed aside all offers from the canal company for its passage through lands under his control. Caspar Wever, developer of the Weverton, Maryland, industrial complex below Harpers Ferry, also had railroad connections. He sought and won high damages for condemnation of his property slated for water-powered milling and manufacturing development. Juries deciding these issues were formed of Maryland citizens natively more sympathetic to the railroad than to the canal. Washington and Allegany county jurors exacted full satisfaction from the canal company on behalf of landowners.

Potomac Valley residents also reaped benefits from the general increase in property values, perhaps the most widely-shared benefit of canal and railroad construction. Property values in Cumberland increased from $931,118 in 1842, the year the railroad arrived, to $2,124,400 in 1860, nine years after the canal reached town. Property values fluctuated with the canal's fortunes, however. Effects of an 1836 work stoppage on the canal on Cumberland were enumerated in a contemporary newspaper account: "The stoppage of the work on the Chesapeake and Ohio Canal has caused a very considerable panic in Cumberland," the paper reported. "Two hours after the arrival of the news, the price of produce came down at least 10 percent." The story went on to lament that ". . . the speculator is cut to the quick, and those who engaged to pay high rents on account of the prospects of the canal, have been suddenly and seriously disappointed. Indeed, the citizens of the town generally, and the farmers for many miles round, have great cause to regret this temporary suspension."

Increased land values resulted from the inexpensive and easy access to principal markets that these commercial arteries brought. In the early 19th century, the ability to transport bulky, heavy goods— the key to both agricultural development and industrialization—could work economic wonders for entire regions. Conversely, its lack could stymie development.

Construction of the canal brought a new class of jobs to the region. When farm work slowed, many inhabitants took canal construction jobs. High demand for many workers where the labor pool was small kept wage rates relatively high throughout the construction period. This occurred despite the importa-

The Canal Water System

The canal was designed to maintain a 2-3-mph current—reducing water resistance—and a depth of 6 feet. To sustain those conditions over 185 miles through widely varying terrain required a finely coordinated hydraulic system. A series of feeder dams **1** impounded the river water to supply the canal, while the guard locks **2** controlled the amount of water entering the system. Culverts **3** carried streams under the canal. Water backing up at lift locks **4** was routed around them through flumes **5**. When the flumes were inadequate, excess water could be drained off to the river through waste weirs **6** by the lockkeeper, who was responsible for the water level below his lock. If heavy flooding threatened the canal, stop locks **7** could divert the water back to the river. In the event of a break in the canal embankment, the stop lock above it could be lowered to confine the loss of water to that section.

The Lockkeeper's Life

He had to be ready "dawn to dawn" to respond to the boatman's horn or shout of "Lock Ready!" and lock the boat through. For his services he received $150 a year (raised to $600 by 1870), a rent-free house, and an acre of land for a garden and livestock. Many keepers supplemented their income by selling produce and bread to the boatmen—and whisky, much to the company's displeasure. One person could operate a lock, but it was more quickly done by two. Other duties came with the job: keepers maintained their locks and were responsible for a stretch of canal below them, repairing leaks and maintaining the correct water level.

Lockkeeper and family, lock 27

Spending much of their lives afloat set canallers apart from the world of permanent homes and unchanging scenery. Their workplace was bounded by the edges of the boat, but ranged over 185 miles. The jargon was semi-nautical: one moved toward the stern, but looked through a window, not a porthole. Before all the boats were supplied by the Canal Towage Co., the owners gave them names like *A. Lincoln, Scow Uncle Sam,* and *Jenny Lind.* The pace of canalling was quite slow—only 2-3 mph—but slow should not be confused with undemanding. One canaller likened it to farm work: "Generally up at daybreak and go to work. About 4 or 5 hours

rest." A full crew consisted of five members: two steersmen, one of whom was the captain; two mule drivers and tenders; and a cook. If the family was large enough, or if the owner could afford hired hands, the boat could operate around the clock with two crews taking 6-hour tricks along with the mule teams. The boats operated from March to December in all kinds of weather. Many canallers had fond memories of their lives on the boats. At 6 or 7 they began to help with the boat, eventually advancing from mule driver to steersman. Boys who chose to stay on the canal often inherited their fathers' boats and became captains.

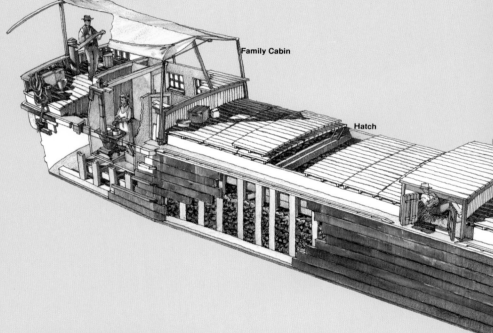

Family Cabin

Hatch

Boat Building

By the canal's most prosperous period in the 1870s, virtually all of the boats were built in Cumberland and were more or less uniform: 90-95 feet long, 14½ feet wide, and drawing 4½ feet when loaded. This was the largest boat the locks could accept.

Several small boatyards built the oak-bottomed, pine-sided boats, which could be expected to last 25 or more years.

Whole families, some of them quite large, lived in the 12x12½-foot cabin. Food was simple but abundant; ham, potatoes, bread, turtle soup, Boatman's Bean Soup, eggs, chicken, fish. Small children played on the cabin roof, tethered for safety. Older children could dive from the roof into a 185-mile swimming hole.

Mules were well-suited to the job: quick learners, steady, sure-footed. Many could be left untended for miles at a stretch. Some even knew when their 6-hour trick was over, pulling up and waiting to be relieved. Most were kept fat, clean, and brushed, and they wore sweat nets to keep off the flies. Few drivers used the whip. A firm "Come Up!" was enough to speed the animals along.

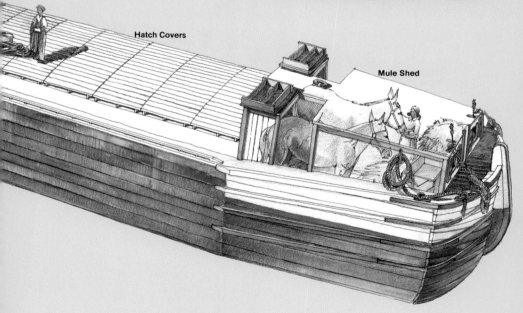

Hatch Covers

Mule Shed

High Water, Hard Times

Most of the canal's shutdowns were caused in one way or another by water: too little water, frozen water, and, worst of all, too much water. Repeated destruction of the canal by floods and consequent disruption of trade was a major reason for its commercial failure. What had made its site so attractive to planners was precisely what made the canal so vulnerable: proximity to the Potomac. Much of the river runs in a narrow bed with steep banks. The canal thus had to be dug close to the river—in some places along a ledge cut into the bank. When heavy rains swelled the river, the canal bore the brunt of its force. Only a year after

1889 flood, lock 33

construction began in 1828, a destructive flood portended things to come. In the flood of 1852, the company had built up the banks, but the river rose 64 feet at Great Falls and did $100,000 worth of damage. The 1889 rainstorm, the same one that flooded Johnstown, Pennsylvania, started the canal's decline. The high waters scattered boats along its length and threw the canal into receivership. The new management repaired the damage, but the canal was already dying when the 1924 flood (below) put it out of business for good. The largest flood on record hit the valley in 1936, putting the canal under 22 feet of water at Shepherdstown.

1902 flood, Snyder's Landing

tion of both unskilled and skilled labor from abroad, a practice that led to many problems and conflicts with local residents. Some valley residents formed construction firms and were awarded contracts to build various canal structures. However, most of the early contracts for major structures were awarded to bidders with previous canal construction experience in New York or Pennsylvania.

Local farmers found a ready market for surplus crops and beverages in the canal construction forces. Lumber was in great demand and so was stone—as ballast, building material, or in the manufacture of hydraulic cement.

Cheap and easier access to markets near the Nation's Capital and Baltimore stimulated Potomac Valley agriculture to diversify. *Niles' Register* for April 9, 1831, reported that, with the opening of the canal between Little Falls and Dam 2 (see map on pages 78 and 79), the cost of shipping a barrel of flour from Little Falls to Georgetown fell from $1 to 30 to 50 cents, and eventually to 7 cents, including tolls. A 10-day period the month before, the paper said, had seen 30,000 barrels of flour descend the waterway. As the canal pushed westward and tapped the rich, grain-producing counties of interior Maryland and southwestern Pennsylvania, trade in these commodities soared. Nearly 280,000 barrels of flour went to market via the canal in the peak year of 1850, and barrels shipped from 1848 to 1853 exceeded 200,000 annually. Large quantities of wheat and corn were also shipped on the canal. Wheat averaged about 225,000 bushels a year between 1842 and 1849, 275,000 bushels a year between 1850 and 1860, and nearly 415,000 a year between 1866 and 1878. The peak year of 1869 saw 605,880 bushels of wheat boated to market on the canal. Corn shipments peaked at 431,760 barrels in 1867. During the Civil War, the railroad captured the flour trade and made Baltimore an international flour shipping port. Canallers never won back that trade.

Victor Cushwa, leading Williamsport merchant and canal shipper, writing in the Hagerstown *Mail* for December 30, 1877, underscored the canal's importance to regional agriculture. The canal was slipping into decline after its most prosperous years. "When our canal was flourishing, until recent years," Cushwa observed, "our farmers within its reach frequently

The Canal Economy

The C&O Canal was a crucial link in an economic web stretching from the mountain town of Cumberland to the tidewater ports of Georgetown and Alexandria—and from there to a broader network of U.S. and trans-Atlantic ports. Existing in a symbiotic relationship with a number of towns, businesses, and industries, the canal depended on their prosperity for its own economic health. A poor crop or a miners' strike meant a loss of revenue from the transport of flour or coal. At the same time, people in canal towns like Hancock, Md., looked to the canal for employment. Regular purchases of food, supplies, and feed by the canallers were also important to the town's economy.

Georgetown was one of the most important elements of the canal economy, for most of the goods shipped by canal were funneled through this port. Tie-ups due to inadequate off-loading facilities, or lack of coasting vessels to accept the loads, could severely slow or even halt canal operations. Georgetown was also the heaviest industrial user of the canal's water. So coveted was the water that Georgetown millers often abused their rights, leaving too little water in the canal for proper navigation. Dependable water for power and inexpensive shipping benefited such industries as the Potomac Granite Co., Potomac Refining Company (lime), and the Round Top Cement Company. Many workers in the Potomac Valley also found employment at the canal boatyards. But it was coal, during the canal's peak years, that became the foundation of the canal economy. Canal towns such as Cumberland, where the coal was loaded, and Williamsport, location of two major coal dealers, prospered as suppliers of coal to a rapidly industrializing nation.

So strong was the network of mines, dealers, canal company, and tidewater shipping that the canal and region at first were little affected by the severe depression of 1873. Not until 1876, as the national demand for coal continued to fall, did the economic crisis catch up with the canal. After that, things were never the same: depression, railroad competition, and floods gradually converted the region's quiet old canal economy into the railroad economy of the new industrial age.

Hancock, Maryland, c. 1900

Canal boat back-up at Georgetown

Potomac Granite Mill, c. 1920

Potomac Refining Company, lime producer

Round Top Cement Mill, early 1900s

Cumberland boat yard

Loading coal at Cumberland

Cushwa coal wharves at Williamsport, 1889

got more for their grain, hay, potatoes, &c than they commanded in Baltimore or other eastern markets, thereby appreciating real-estate, private and public wealth. . . ."

After damages resulting from the 1889 flood closed the canal, Cushwa wrote again: "Loss of business, labor and property amounting to hundreds of thousands of dollars. . . most seriously affect the prosperity of the people of Western Maryland, to so many of whom the canal was the only market and sole artery of trade." Cushwa also observed that the canal was a consumer of produce as well as a carrier of it, with boatmen liberal buyers of farm products.

Another boon to agriculture resulted from the economical shipment of fertilizers on the canal. Peruvian guano helped rejuvenate lands that, by the 1830s, had been ruined by tobacco farming. These were restored to cereals and grasses after 1845 in a program fostered by the Society of Friends and the Virginia Society for the Advancement of Agriculture.

Milling and manufacturing were promoted throughout the Potomac Valley by the canal's sale of water-power as well as by its transportation facilities. Canal officials first thought that small manufacturing villages would spring up all along the line, producing double profits as the canal would both sell water-power and transport resulting goods. Other authorities said, accurately, that manufacturing would develop only near towns, but canal officers touted their notion into the 1870s. Water-powered mills, foundries, and textile operations developed principally at or near Hancock, Williamsport, Weverton, and Georgetown. Georgetown offered good opportunities for milling and manufacturing because it was both port city and trade center near markets, labor supplies, and capital. The canal company never reaped great profits from water rights sales, but in some years such sales were its *only* source of income.

By far the biggest economic factor for both canal and railroad was Cumberland coal. As canal and railroad competed for profitable freight rates, mine owners and operators increased their profits even more. Between 1842 and 1877, the canal and railroad transported nearly 32 million tons of coal, one-third by canal and two-thirds by rail. In its peak coal-trade year of 1875, the canal carried 904,898 tons. Benefits to Cumberland coal economics are readily illustrated: in 1842, the year that the B&O Railroad reached Cumberland, only 1,078 tons of coal were transported over its line. By the time the canal reached Cumberland in 1850, the railroad was shipping 192,806 tons. In 1873, the peak year for Cumberland coal shipments, nearly 2.7 million tons went to market. After the 1889 flood put the canal into receivership, it carried coal cargoes almost exclusively.

Canal-related industries supported many families in the Potomac Valley. Boatbuilding and repair became a profitable occupation. Eight principal firms were engaged in canal boat construction and maintenance in the early 1870s. All but one, at Hancock, were located in Cumberland. At least seven dry docks were built along the waterway for boat repairs. Many people made comfortable livings from grocery and feed store operations along the waterway. Merchants provisioned boatmen, families, and their mules. There were at least 27 grocery and feed stores between Lock 6 at Little Falls and Oldtown. Mules were considerable consumers. In 1873, a Williamsport newspaper observed that "The Chesapeake & Ohio Canal employs 400 boats constantly during the boating season. These boats require 2,000 head of mules, and give employment to 2,000 persons directly and 2,000 indirectly. The mules consume at least 25,000 barrels of corn; 3,840 bushels of oats, and 500 tons of hay. This provender, which is mainly purchased along the line of the canal, costs in the aggregate $60,000."

Profits also accrued to the Potomac Valley from shipping lines that called at Georgetown wharves. Ships carried the Cumberland region's hard supercoal to New England textile mills and iron smelting operations. During the 1850s and mid-1870s, Cumberland coal was also shipped to East Coast port cities, the British West Indies, and the northern coast of South America.

One canal-related economic activity particularly irked canal officials. Transferring goods proved more profitable than shipping them, and the canal company resented the profits of canal wharf and warehousing operations. Canal officials complained that "in 1874 the boatmen received for their services $1,070,000, the wharf owners $344,000, while the canal company received from tolls on coal and boats but $428,000 for maintaining and operating a work which cost over $11,000,000. . . ." Wharf owners reaped their

profits on investments of about $300,000, which the canal company found unfair.

The most important way in which the Potomac Valley was influenced by the canal's construction was in financial affairs. Sizable canal and railroad payrolls, most spent in immediate neighborhoods, fed valley prosperity. Cycles of optimism and pessimism, of boom and gloom, therefore rose and fell with the fortunes of the canal and railroad.

One particularly significant contribution of the canal to valley economic life was the company's issuance of scrip. During the progress of their works both the railroad and the canal resorted to the issuance of their own paper money at various times. To prevent a work stoppage while bonds were funded, the canal company first issued scrip in 1834, about $90,000 worth in $5, $10, and $20 notes. Acute currency shortages after the financial Panic of 1837 gave the canal company another excuse to issue scrip—$50,000 worth in denominations from 50 cents to $5. These early issues of scrip were desperately needed in a currency-starved region. Subsequent canal and railroad issues of scrip were not so well received. Doubt about the companies' own fiscal health caused the scrips, used to pay employee wages, to be heavily discounted.

Despite such fluctuating fortunes as its history of scrip issuance symbolizes, the C&O Canal persistently served to stimulate Potomac Valley life from its optimistic outset in 1828 to its demise by flooding in 1924. While we may fairly deem the canal a disappointment for its investors, the Great National Project originally envisioned was in many ways realized. It served its region well for nearly a century. Nor should we give short shrift to the canal's continuing contributions. Capital expenditures of a mere $11 million more than a century and a half ago produced for us an invaluable and quite unforeseen legacy. Today, the canal and its towpath offer unparalleled opportunities for outdoor recreation in the Potomac Valley. From tidewater at Georgetown to the Alleghenies, the C&O Canal is now a pathway to inner wealth.

Cement was one of many heavy commodities critical to early economic development that were shipped cost effectively on canals. Round Top Cement Mill hugged the C&O Canal north of Hancock, Md. It is shown above in ruins today and, on the facing page, after operations had ceased with the closing of the canal.

Stone and Stone Cutting

The quarry and stone-cutting industry along the Potomac River predated the C&O Canal, but the efficient means of transport provided by the canal spurred the growth of the industry. The canal itself depended on stone. The "masses" of usable stone early surveyors for the project had found along the canal were crucial to the success of the venture. Limestone and sandstone were used in most of the locks, aqueducts, and other structures on the canal, with granite often used below Harpers Ferry. Some of the best stone was found at Seneca Red Sandstone Quarries, near the mouth of Seneca Creek. The quarry had been a source of widely-used Seneca Red Stone since before the Revolution, and it supplied stone for many of the locks between #8 and #27, and for Aqueduct #1 over Seneca Creek. While fresh from the quarry the stone was soft with what the workers called "quarry sap" and could easily be cut and carved, but with weathering it became hard and durable. Taking advantage of this quality, the Seneca Sandstone Company in 1837 built a mill (below) near the quarry to cut the stone. The mill was a major operation; besides cutting Seneca Red Stone, it cut stone from other quarries for use in such structures as the U.S. Capitol and the Washington Monument.

Stonecutting Mill

Stone Polishers

Quarry

Stone Saws

Loading Canal Boat

Drilling Stone

Seneca Red Stone was widely desired for its rich color, fine grain, and durability. It was used in the Smithsonian Castle on the Mall (left), in the Cabin John aqueduct-bridge—when built the longest single span arch in the world—and in the period's ubiquitous brownstone houses.

Mule-drawn railway cars carried large pieces of sandstone from Seneca Quarries to the cutting mill. Workers shaped the stone with hammer and chisel, then cut it into blocks with a water-powered reciprocal saw. The motion of the toothless blade in a water/sand mixture cut the block—about an inch an hour.

Cutting Stone

Workers at Seneca Stone Cutting Mill, around 1890.

Ironmaking

During the years when every eastern state seemed to be building its own canal, the centuries-old technologies of ironmaking and canal building depended on each other. With the United States on the verge of its industrial revolution, however, their futures were very different. The days of canal transport were numbered, while the iron and steel industry would expand rapidly and grow more sophisticated, providing the basic material of the industrial age. But in the first half of the 19th century, American ironmakers still furnished the hardware for stone and wood structures, such as canals. The Chesapeake and Ohio Canal and

the iron furnaces at Cumberland, Sharpsburg, Georgetown, and other towns along the Potomac proved mutually beneficial. To the ironmasters, the canal was a godsend, as their extremely heavy products were much less expensive to transport on the canal than over rough and undependable roads. Some furnaces and foundries bought water from the canal company to drive their waterwheels. The canal company, for its part, needed wrought and cast iron hardware for the lock gates. Even before the canal was built, the Potomac Valley attracted iron manufacturers. The raw materials of ironmaking—iron ore, limestone, and charcoal—

Tunnel Head

Molten Iron
and Slag

Bosh

Crucible

Cast Arch

Hearth

Tuyere

Pig Bed

Slag

were available in the area, and there was plenty of falling water to power the blast furnaces. The process itself was simple. Layers of ore, limestone (the flux that removed impurities from the ore), and charcoal were dumped into the top of the furnace and heated until the melted iron ran to the bottom and was tapped. Much of it was channeled directly into shallow grooves, where it hardened into pig iron, the form in which most iron was shipped.

The Versatile Metal

The pig iron bar produced by the blast furnace was raw material for casting or forging. If shipped to a foundry, it was remelted and cast in molds (below left). Cast iron, relatively high in carbon and thus hard, was good for producing objects of a precise weight or shape, such as a scale weight or a valve for a canal gate. It was also used for items that had to withstand great heat, such as cooking pots. Pig iron was also shipped to forges, where it was converted to wrought iron. The bars were heated in a charcoal fire to burn off some of the carbon. The pulpy mass (below) was then put under a large hammer (above) to beat out impurities.

Pig Iron

Wrought Iron Bar

The **iron** was reheated and beaten several times to lengthen and toughen the fibers.

The final product was a merchant bar sold to mills or blacksmiths. Because wrought iron contained less carbon, it was softer and less brittle in its cold state than cast iron. It was beaten or rolled and cut into shape rather than melted and cast.

Blowing Tubs

Blast Machinery

As the **blacksmith** beat out the bar iron, he continued the process begun in the forge. He drew out the fibers in the metal, aligning them so the final product would be tough and resilient, as an ax blade or a sluice valve handle had to be.

The Race West

From the start the C&O had unwelcome company in its reach for western markets. On July 4, 1828, the day the canal was inaugurated, ground was broken for the Baltimore and Ohio Railroad, the first profit-making railroad in America. The B&O reached Cumberland and the lucrative coal-carrying trade 8 years before the canal. The competition lasted for almost 60 years, with the railroad always a step ahead. The ancient canal technology was destined to lose in the end to the symbol of the new industrial age. When the canal company was devastated by the 1889 flood, control passed to the principal bondholder: its old adversary, the B&O Railroad.

"The Rivals" shows canal horse spooked by a locomotive. Below: A B&O train passes a C&O boat near Harpers Ferry, West Virginia, 1920.

America's first canal was built in 1786, its earliest revenue-producing railroad in 1830. Before the first locomotive rolled, there were 1,200 miles of canals. Despite the canals' 44-year head start, by mid-century there were twice as many miles of railroad track. Canal abandonments were exceeding construction. Why did railroads so quickly displace canals? They were faster and, with consolidation, less expensive and more efficient. But it was dependability that gave railroads the upper hand. They kept rolling year round, while ice, drought, and floods closed the canals. By the Civil War the railroads had won the western markets.

Railroad system in 1850

Canal system in 1850

Part 3

Guide and Adviser

Approaching the Canal

The C&O Canal stretches along the Potomac River's Maryland shore from the mouth of Rock Creek at tidewater in Georgetown to Cumberland, Maryland. It gains 605 feet in elevation from its tide lock to its western terminus beneath the Allegheny Mountains. Maps on pages 78, 84, and 92 show access roads along the canal's length. Major feeder highways to canal access roads are—from east to west—Capital Beltway, I-495; 1-270 from below Rockville to Frederick; I-70 from Frederick to Hancock; and I-68 from Hancock to Cumberland. The maps also show Potomac River bridges that give access to the canal from Virginia and West Virginia. Whites Ferry (toll auto ferry) serves motorists crossing the river between Route 15 north of Leesburg, Virginia and Poolesville, Maryland, via Route 107.

Visitor Centers. The National Park Service operates visitor centers at Georgetown, Great Falls (in the tavern building), Brunswick, Williamsport, Hancock, and Cumberland. Canal headquarters are in Hagerstown, Maryland (see below).

For General Canal Information. Contact:
C&O Canal National Historical Park
1850 Dual Highway, Suite 100
Hagerstown, MD 21740
301-739-4200, V/TDD
e-mail choh_information@nps.gov
www.nps.gov/choh
    For information on the canal in **Georgetown** contact:
Georgetown Visitor Center
1057 Thomas Jefferson Street, NW
Washington, DC 20007
202-653-5190
Maps, books, and tickets for canal boat rides in Georgetown are sold here.

For information about the **Great Falls**, Maryland, area or the section from Georgetown to Edwards Ferry, contact the canal visitor center in:
Great Falls Tavern
11710 MacArthur Blvd.
Potomac, MD 20854.
301-267-3714, V/TDD
Buy maps, books, and tickets for Great Falls canal boat rides here. An exhibit in the Crommelin House on canal life has a model of a lock with boats.

For information on the canal in the **Brunswick area** visit the Brunswick Museum at 40 West Potomac Street in Brunswick.

For information on the canal from **Edwards Ferry to Big Pool**, phone 301-582-0813, V/TDD. The Williamsport Visitor Center is in the Cushwa Basin area of the canal. Exhibits describe canal life and commerce. Maps and books on canal history and the Williamsport area are sold here.

For information on the canal from **Big Pool to the Paw Paw Tunnel**, call 301-678-5463, V/TDD. The Hancock Visitor Center is on the main street through Hancock. Exhibits describe canal construction and the industries of the Hancock area.

For information on the canal from the **Paw Paw Tunnel to Cumberland**, phone 301-722-8226, V/TDD. Exhibits describe canal life, boat building and coal mining. Books and maps of the canal and environs are sold here.
    More canal information centers are listed on pages 106 and 107

Canal Boat Rides. From mid-April to mid-October, canal boat rides are offered at Georgetown and Great Falls. Relive the canal's most prosperous era—the 1870s—as you pass through a lock and ride the flatwater powered by mules. Boat captain, crews, and mule tenders in period dress narrate your trip, sing canal songs, and share lore about boating days. You can learn a lot about what life was like for typical canal boating families more than 100 years ago.

There is a fee for both boat trips: Tickets are sold the day of the trip at the Georgetown Visitor Center and Great Falls Tavern Visitor Center: Organized groups can make reservations or arrange evening trips.

For information about trips on *The Georgetown* call 202-653-5190 V/TDD. For information about trips at Great Falls call 301-767-3714 V/TDD.

Canal boat rides today

Nearby Park Areas. Park areas adjoining the C&O Canal or Potomac River can make enjoyable side trips from the canal. **Rock Creek Park** heads inland from the canal's Georgetown terminus. Dating from 1890 it is one of the Nation's earliest large city parks, and it adjoins the **National Zoological Park** of the Smithsonian Institution. **Great Falls Park.** On the Virginia side of the Potomac, opposite the canal, Great Falls Park offers scenic vistas of the river where it tumbles over a steep, jagged rock wall and flows through a narrow gorge. **(On the Maryland shore a footbridge provides access to stunning vistas of the falls.)** Great Falls Park also preserves canal works of The Patowmack Company (see Part 1). **Goose Creek** *(Virginia)* **State Scenic River** preserves former dam sites and locks of the Goose Creek and Little River Navigation in Loudoun County opposite Edwards Ferry (see map on pages 84 and 85). **Harpers Ferry National Historical Park**—see pages 90 and 92. For information on **Antietam National Battlefield**, see page 87, and **Fort Frederick State Park**, see page 94.

Ferry Hill Plantation

Today's Cumberland skyline

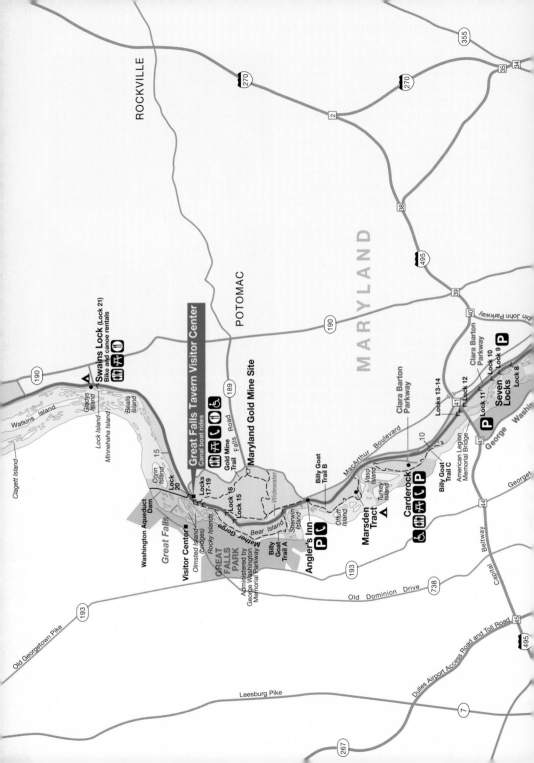

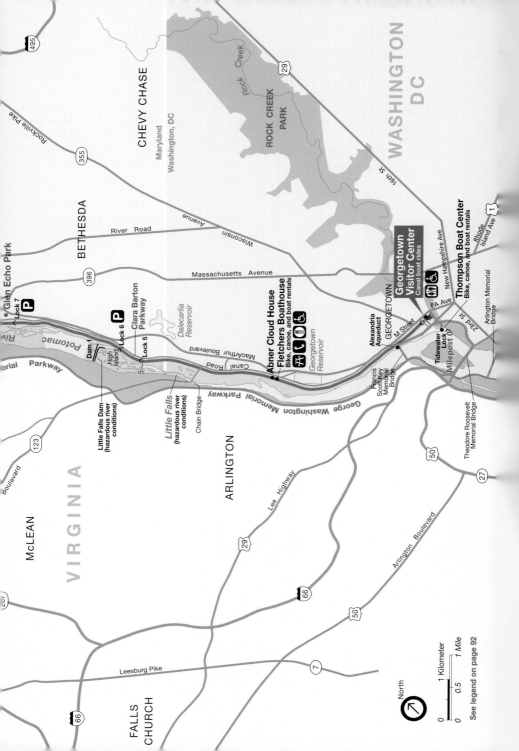

WASHINGTON DC

ROCK CREEK PARK

Rock Creek

Maryland
Washington, DC

29

16th St

CHEVY CHASE

355

BETHESDA

River   Road

396

Wisconsin   Avenue

Massachusetts   Avenue

Rockville Pike

Glen Echo Park

Lock 7

Lock 6

Clara Barton Parkway

Dam 1

High Island

Lock 5

Canal Road

MacArthur Boulevard

Dalecarlia Reservoir

Georgetown Reservoir

Abner Cloud House
Fletchers Boathouse
Bike, canoe, and boat rentals

**Georgetown
Visitor Center**
Canal boat rides

GEORGETOWN

New Hampshire Ave

Thompson Boat Center
Bike, canoe, and boat rentals

Rhode Island Ave

1

Alexandria Aqueduct

M Street

PA Ave

Tidewater Lock

Milepost 0

22nd St

Arlington Memorial Bridge

Francis Scott Key Memorial Bridge

Theodore Roosevelt Memorial Bridge

50

27

Potomac River

emorial   Parkway

George Washington Memorial Parkway

Little Falls Dam
(hazardous river conditions)

Little Falls
(hazardous river conditions)

Chain Bridge

VIRGINIA

McLEAN

123

Boulevard

ARLINGTON

Lee Highway

29

66

50

Arlington   Boulevard

FALLS CHURCH

Leesburg Pike

7

66

495

North

0   1 Kilometer
0   0.5   1 Mile

See legend on page 92

Georgetown. Lower Georgetown affords one of the most concentrated series of locks on the canal. In less than one-half mile, Locks 1 through 4 lift the canal up from its tidelock and the Rock Creek basin for passage through historic Georgetown. An early, thriving tidal port for the East Coast and Europe trades, Georgetown predated the Nation's Capital.

Thompson's Boat Center. For information about boat, canoe, and bicycle rentals here, see Recreation, pages 98-100.

Alexandria Aqueduct. Just upstream of Key Bridge, on the river side of the towpath, are the remains of the 1,100-foot-long Alexandria Aqueduct, **Milepost 1.** Written up in engineering journals of its day, the aqueduct carried canal boats across the Potomac River to a 7-mile-long branch canal whose tidelock lay in Alexandria. This canal opened in 1843 and diverted substantial port trade from Georgetown. At that time, Georgetown's low bridges prevented passage of the large canal boats that had evolved since the C&O Canal opened. Georgetown's bridges were raised after the Civil War, during which the aqueduct was converted to a troop and vehicle bridge. The aqueduct was put back into use in 1868, with a toll highway bridge built over the trough. This was replaced by an iron-truss bridge after 1886.

Georgetown Canal Incline. Only granite slabs and bits of iron remain of the incline plane that lowered boats from the canal to the river here, **Milepost 2.** Completed in 1876 and acclaimed at the 1878 Paris Exposition, it was built to solve long tie-ups of boat traffic at Georgetown. The incline lowered canal boats 300 feet to the river. Tugboats towed them to the Navy Yard, Alexandria, and other points.

Fletcher's Boathouse. For information about boat, canoe, and bicycle rentals here, see Recreation, pages 98-100.

Abner Cloud House. Situated just above Fletcher's Boathouse, the Abner Cloud House, **Milepost 3,** is the oldest existing structure on the canal. It was completed in 1801. Cloud operated a mill, storing grain and flour in the house's basement. The Colonial Dames of America, Chapter III, shares the house with the park and conducts interpretive programs. From here upstream to Lock 5 much of the canal lies in the bed of the Patowmack Company's Little Falls Skirting Canal. The first of the inlet locks admitting river water diverted from behind Dam 1 into the canal is located next to Lock 5. One-half mile upriver, the Potomac's Little Falls marks the end of tidal influence.

Glen Echo Park and Clara Barton House. Glen Echo Park, just above Lock 7, **Milepost 7,** began as the site of the National Chautauqua and was later made into an amusement park. Now managed by the National Park Service, it serves as the site of cultural, educational, and recreational programs. The National Park Service also manages the home of Clara Barton, who founded the American Red Cross. It lies just upstream of Glen Echo.

Cabin John Bridge. Just up Cabin John Creek, the stunning single-span stone arch Cabin John Bridge, **Milepost 7,** carries MacArthur Boulevard and a water conduit over the creek's deep valley. At its completion in 1864, it was the longest stone arch in the world. Canal boats hauled the Seneca red sandstone of its parapets down from nearby Seneca. Schooners brought the granite forming the arch from Quincy, Massachusetts, to Potomac tidewater. Canal boats hauled them to the site.

Seven Locks. Locks 8 through 14

make up the Seven Locks that raise the canal 56 feet in just 1.25 miles, **Mileposts 8 and 9.** Locks 9, 10, and 12 are equipped with drop gates rather than swing gates to speed passage through this series of locks. Construction of Lock House 6, at Lock 8, was completed in the spring of 1830. (See pages 54-55 for lock house illustration.)

Widewater. A favored stretch among anglers and canoeists, Widewater, **Milepost 12,** marks where canal engineers opted to use an old river channel rather than build a new canal in the cliffs. An apparent small lake results, some 400 feet wide and less than 1 mile long. Trails to the spectacular river bluffs and views of Mather Gorge below Great Falls tie in to the towpath here. **Warning:** these rough, often steep, and rocky trails require stamina and sturdy footgear.

Six Locks. At the head of Widewater Lock 15 begins the Six Locks grouped in 1 mile and including Lock 20 at Great Falls Tavern. A **stop lock** between Locks 16 and 17 could form a wooden dam across the canal and towpath to protect lower parts of the canal from flood damage. A levee shunted stopped floodwaters back to the river channel.

Great Falls Tavern. The visitor center is located in the Great Falls Tavern building, **Milepost 14** (see pages 88-89). For information about **boat rides at Great Falls,** call 301-299-2026, or ask at the visitor center. For the hearing impaired call 301-299-3613, V/TDD.

Swains Lock. Lock 21 is named for the Swains, a family associated with the canal since its construction. A Swain tended this lock, **Milepost 16,** when the canal shut down in 1924, and Swains still live in the lockkeeper's house. (See pages 98-100 for bicycle and canoe rental information.)

Canoeing at Georgetown

Photographing fall colors

Winter envelopes Lock No. 8

Georgetown, the canal's tidewater terminus, had been a port for more than 150 years when the canal was completed, and in 1850 Georgetown still maintained its charter as an independent town. In the late 18th century, flour from the port's mills had been shipped around the world. In those prosperous times, Georgetown and the rival port of Alexandria, Virginia, hoped to compete with the major northern ports, but the deeper harbors required by larger steam vessels and the advent of the railroads relegated these Potomac River ports to secondary status. The C&O Canal gave Georgetown the

boost it needed. Countless tons of coal, flour, and lumber moved through the town, and the abundant water-power furnished by the closely-spaced locks furthered industrial growth. To most canallers Georgetown was a welcome sight at the end of their 185-mile trip—their connection to the larger world. Some canal families did all their shopping for the year in Georgetown. Children had access to ice cream; adults to beer. They could even buy ice from the same New England schooners (below) that would carry their coal northward.

Canal boats bound for **Alexandria** crossed the Potomac River on the 1,100-foot Alexandria Aqueduct, opened in 1843. When the boats reached Alexandria, they were lowered into the Potomac through four lift locks. The aqueduct survived as a bridge until it was replaced by the Key Bridge in 1933.

So busy was **Georgetown** during the canal's prime that boatmen often got caught in tie-ups, waiting in lines sometimes 5 miles long for 4 or 5 days before being cleared through. Georgetown is still a vital part of Washington, known for its shops, nightlife, and Georgetown University. In the midst of this bustling urban community, the canal provides a place for quiet walks and summertime concerts.

Pierre L'Enfant's 1791 plan for the new capital called for a canal that, from Tiber Creek, would run along what is now Constitution Avenue, turn south in front of the Capitol, then divide, one branch to terminate at the Navy Yard on the Anacostia River, the other at Greenleaf Point.

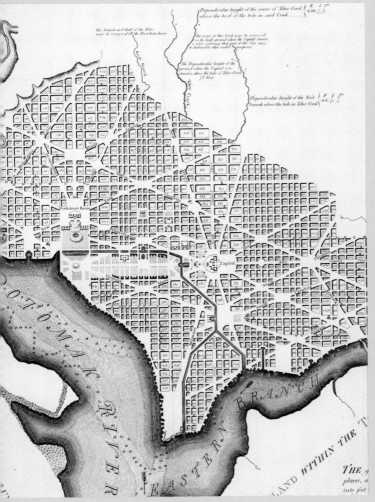

When the C&O Canal Company was chartered, the **Washington Canal** had been in operation since 1815. Developers hoped it would help Washington become an entrepot, while allowing boats to avoid the hazardous trip around Greenleaf Point to the Navy Yard. But the canal had been plagued with poor design, silting, and lack of capital. It was given a second chance when the C&O built its Washington Extension between the Rock Creek tidal lock and the Washington Canal's entrance at Tiber Creek in 1833. The completion of the Alexandria Canal in 1843 gave boatmen several alternatives. They could unload in Georgetown; lock into the river and move their load to a vessel at Georgetown; continue to Washington and unload there; take the Alexandria Canal to that port; or be towed to downriver ports. The Washington Canal thrived for a while, but continued silting closed it in the 1870s. The Alexandria Canal operated until 1886, when the aqueduct was converted into a bridge.

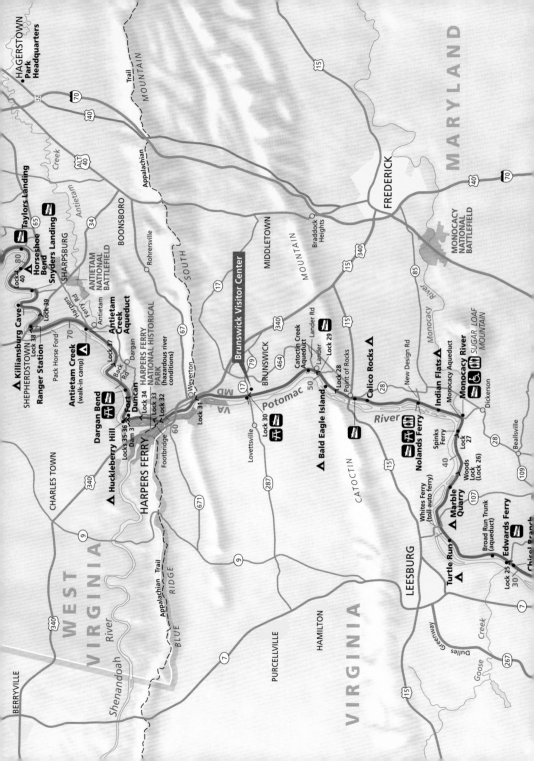

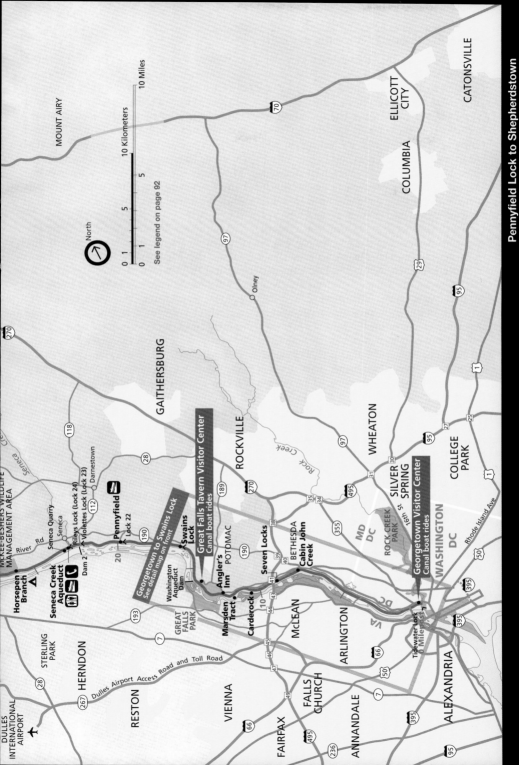

MOUNT AIRY

North

10 Kilometers
0 1   5   10 Kilometers
0 1   5   10 Miles

See legend on page 92

70

97

Olney

29

95

11

GAITHERSBURG

ROCKVILLE

WHEATON

COLUMBIA

ELLICOTT CITY

CATONSVILLE

97

SILVER SPRING

31
16th St

COLLEGE PARK

11

25

95

27

30

495

355

35
34

ROCK CREEK PARK

Rock Creek

MD
DC

WASHINGTON DC

Rhode Island Ave

50

270

118

28

Darnestown

112

Seneca
Seneca Quarry
River Rd.

McKEE-BESHERS WILDLIFE MANAGEMENT AREA

Seneca

Horsepen Branch

Seneca Creek Aqueduct

270

28

STERLING PARK

DULLES INTERNATIONAL AIRPORT

HERNDON

267

7

RESTON

193

GREAT FALLS PARK

VIENNA

66

FAIRFAX

FALLS CHURCH

495

ANNANDALE

236

7

McLEAN

ARLINGTON

66

50

VA

395

ALEXANDRIA

95

395

Tidewater Lock
(1 Mile)

Georgetown Visitor Center
Canal boat rides

DC

Cabin John Creek

BETHESDA

Seven Locks

190

38
39
40
41
42
43
44
45
46
47
49

Carderock

10

Marsden Tract

Angler's Inn

POTOMAC

Washington Aqueduct Dam

Great Falls Tavern Visitor Center
Canal boat rides

Georgetown to Swains Lock
See detail map on front

Swains Lock

20

Lock 22

Pennyfield

Violettes Lock (Lock 23)

Rileys Lock (Lock 24)

Dam 2

189

118

Pennyfield Lock to Shepherdstown

Pennyfield Lock. President Grover Cleveland loved to fish for bass near Pennyfield Lock, **Milepost 19.** He often stayed in the Pennyfield's inn on the canal's berm side (not in the lock house) and dined with them. Birdwatchers find many species of birds, including ducks, frequenting these canal and river environs. Upstream lie the Marshall Bidwell Wildlife Management Area and a sandstone culvert (see pages 36 and 37) with 16-foot span and 8-foot rise. Culverts far outnumbered locks and aqueducts combined, representing a major engineering and construction challenge.

Violettes Lock. Violettes Lock marks the head of the major watered section of today's canal, **Milepost 22.** The adjoining inlet lock provides river water, diverted from behind Dam 2, for the canal between here and Dam 1 at Little Falls. Boats could also pass between canal and river through this lock.

Seneca Creek Aqueduct. The combined lift lock and Seneca Creek Aqueduct and the lock house, **Milepost 23,** were built of Seneca red sandstone quarried here and cut and dressed at the Seneca stone cutting mill (see pages 68 and 69). Its ruins lie just upstream on the inland side of the canal.

Wildlife Area. McKee Besher Wildlife Management Area protects habitat for many species of wildlife on the Maryland side where the river boasts sizable Van Deventer and Selden islands, **Milepost 26.**

Edwards Ferry and Lock 25. Edwards Ferry operated on the river from 1791 to 1836. Today there is a river boat ramp here, **Milepost 30,** with road access across the lock by the ruins of Jarboes Store, which supplied the boating trade and the local community. Lock 25 was the first lock to be lengthened so that two canal boats could lock through at once.

Whites Ferry. Whites Ferry (fee), the last operating ferry on the Potomac, carries vehicles across the Potomac above **Milepost 35,** keeping alive a 150-year tradition. Troops used the ferry and river crossing here during the Civil War. Several Indian villages were located on river flats and bluffs in this vicinity. The ferry provides access to the historic Leesburg, Virginia, area and Balls Bluff National Cemetery, site of a Civil War Battle.

Monocacy River Aqueduct. Perhaps the most beautiful structure on the canal, the Monocacy River Aqueduct carried the waterway over the Monocacy River, **Milepost 42.** White and pink quartz sandstones used to build the aqueduct were quarried at the base of nearby Sugarloaf Mountain and hauled here by wagon or by boat down the Monocacy, or via a wooden-railed tramway built for the project. Confederate troops attempted to blow up this aqueduct during the Civil War, but its sound masonry defied their efforts.

Point of Rocks. Canal construction halted for 4 years at Point of Rocks in a right-of-way dispute with the railroad: there was room for only one of them where Catoctin Mountain comes down to the Potomac, **Milepost 49.** The railroad tunneled through the mountain but laid track atop the canal in the 1960s. The picturesque railway station here is on the National Register of Historic Places. Confederate troops destroyed the original Lock 28, upstream, in 1862. U.S. Route 15 crosses the Potomac River bridge here. There is a river boat ramp just downstream.

Brunswick. Brunswick is a railroad town complete with a private railroad museum downtown, **Milepost 55.** The B&O located its eastern switching yard here in 1890. Commuters account for most passenger train use today. Ferry services preceded the bridges here. Earlier bridges were destroyed in the Civil War and the 1936 flood.

Weverton. An extensive manufacturing center planned and built in the 1830s near today's Lock 31 at Weverton, **Milepost 58,** hoped to rival Lowell, Massachusetts, as a center of industry. Entrepreneur Caspar Wever had worked on construction of both the National Road and the B&O Railroad. The Potomac's 15-foot fall below Harpers Ferry promised ample water power. Wever died before his hopes bore fruit, but the town became a significant manufacturing center—cotton mill, file factory, and marble works—for a time.

Harpers Ferry. The footbridge on the railroad bridge provides passage between the canal and Harpers Ferry, **Milepost 60.** (See pages 90 to 91 for Harpers Ferry information.) The footbridge also carries the Appalachian Trail, which stretches from Maine to Georgia, across the Potomac River. The Shenandoah River Lock, downstream from Lock 33, was the first river lock built. It was soon abandoned in favor of the river lock at Lock 35.

Antietam Creek Aqueduct. The bloodiest day of the Civil War occurred on September 17, 1862, near Antietam Creek, **Milepost 69.** Some 23,000 soldiers were killed or wounded in one day. Nearby Antietam National Battlefield, also managed by the National Park Service, commemorates the tragedy. The Park Service has a canal information center at Antietam Creek.

Shepherdstown Area. Near the railroad bridge piers, a river lock passed boats between the river and canal, **Milepost 72.** Shepherdstown was an important trade and manufacturing center when the canal was built. Limestone for its early masonry works came from a mill just below the town.

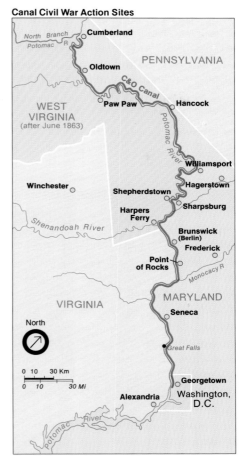

Canal Civil War Action Sites

Paralleling the Potomac River boundary between North and South and serving as a supply line for Washington, D.C., the canal saw considerable Civil War action along its length. Confederate troops repeatedly tried to disable its aqueducts and the feeder dams on the river. Control of industrial Harpers Ferry, located at the confluence of the Shenandoah and Potomac rivers, passed back and forth between North and South early in the Civil War.

Great Falls and Its Tavern

Where the Potomac makes its sharpest drop at Great Falls, we are given a spectacular demonstration of the river's power. It is a place of raw beauty, as the river surges through narrow chutes and spills over huge rocks, then cuts deep into the bedrock below the falls, creating Mather Gorge. Six locks were required to drop canal boats 41 feet in less than a mile. At the uppermost lock, the lockkeeper's house built in 1829 was enlarged twice by 1831. With the expansion, it was known as Crommelin House, a popular hotel operating through the 19th century and the center of a thriving community at Great Falls.

Even before the canal opened, Washingtonians headed for Great Falls on outings. Congressmen and high officials were among those for whom the hotel was a favorite haunt. The canallers were not impressed with the spot's charms, complaining that the tourists interfered with locking through.

Industrial Harpers Ferry

Harpers Ferry's dramatic natural setting matches its historical significance. The town sits astride the point where the Shenandoah River joins the Potomac and both cut sharply through the Blue Ridge. The settlement was named after Robert Harper, who in 1747 ran a ferry there. Recognizing its natural advantages—water power, transportation, and a thriving iron industry upriver—George Washington recommended in 1795 that a national armory be established at Harpers Ferry. By 1803, the armory was producing muskets, and later, in the first practical demonstration of mass production, the Hall Rifle Works turned out excellent breech-loading rifles.

The coming of the C&O Canal and the B&O Railroad in the 1830s confirmed the town's importance and ushered in its peak years. It was a smoky and rambunctious industrial town of 3,000, its hills denuded of trees to feed the industry. But the Civil War soured the town's brief taste of prosperity. Troops from both sides took turns occupying the town, and the Union army burned the arsenal and armory in 1861 to keep it out of Confederate hands. After the war, floods dealt the town a series of blows from which it never recovered. Today, restored buildings and history programs help recreate the 19th-century mood of this industrial town.

John Brown was a fervent abolitionist who planned to liberate slaves. He seized the armory at Harpers Ferry in October 1859, intending to equip a guerrilla army, but was captured in the firehouse in which he and his men had barricaded themselves. He was convicted of murder and treason and hanged on December 2.

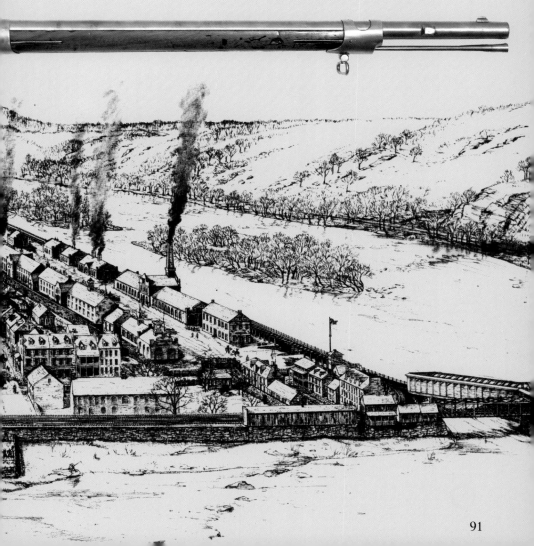

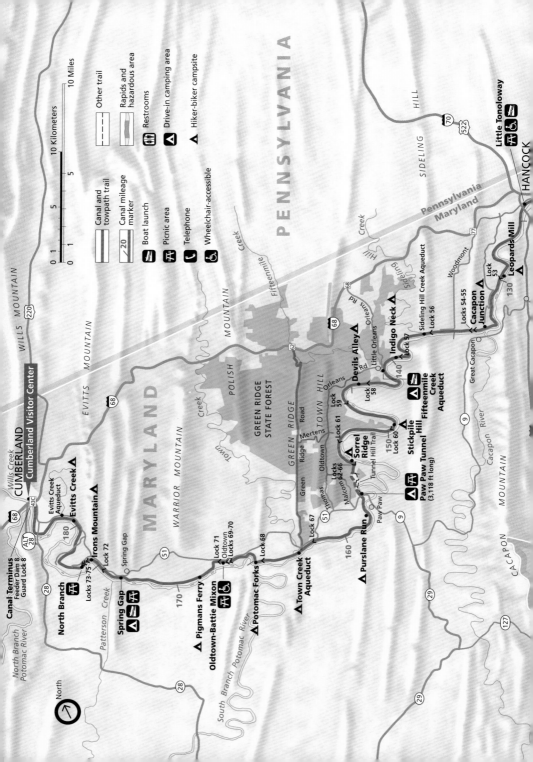

North

CUMBERLAND

Canal Terminus
Feeder Dam 8
Guard Lock 8

Evitts Creek
Aqueduct
Evitts Creek ▲

North Branch 🏕

Locks 73-75

Lock 72

Spring Gap

Spring Gap ▲🏕

Irons Mountain ▲

Irons Mountain ▲

▲ **Pigmans Ferry**

Oldtown-Battie Mixon 🏕♿

Lock 71
Oldtown
Locks 69-70

Lock 68

▲ **Potomac Forks**

▲ **Town Creek Aqueduct**

Lock 67

Malcom

Thomas

▲ **Purslane Run**

Paw Paw

Paw Paw Tunnel Hill
(3,118 ft long) 🏕🏕

Locks 62-66

Tunnel Hill Trail

▲ **Sorrel Ridge**

Lock 61

Mertens

Green
Ridge
Road

Lock 60

▲ **Stickpile Hill**

Fifteenmile Creek Aqueduct 🏕

Lock 59

Lock 58

Oldtown

Devils Alley ▲

Little Orleans

Orleans

Orleans Rd

Lock 57

Indigo Neck ▲

Lock 56

Sideling Hill Creek Aqueduct

Locks 54-55

▲ **Cacapon Junction**

Lock 53

Leopards Mill ▲

Little Tonoloway 🏕♿

HANCOCK

Woodmont

GREEN RIDGE STATE FOREST

POLISH MOUNTAIN

GREEN RIDGE

TOWN HILL

SIDELING HILL

EVITTS MOUNTAIN

WARRIOR MOUNTAIN

WILLS MOUNTAIN

CACAPON MOUNTAIN

PENNSYLVANIA

MARYLAND

Pennsylvania
Maryland

North Branch Potomac River

South Branch Potomac River

Patterson Creek

Town Creek

Fifteenmile Creek

Sideling Hill Creek

Cacapon River

Great Cacapon

Wills Creek

180
170
160
150
140
130

Map legend:

- Canal and towpath trail
- Canal mileage marker — 20
- 🚤 Boat launch
- 🏕 Picnic area
- ☎ Telephone
- ♿ Wheelchair-accessible
- Other trail
- Rapids and hazardous area
- 🚻 Restrooms
- 🏕 Drive-in camping area
- ▲ Hiker-biker campsite

Scale:
10 Miles
10 Kilometers
0 1 5 10

220
43C
ALT 28
28
68
51
68
62
68
9
29
127
70
522
77
9

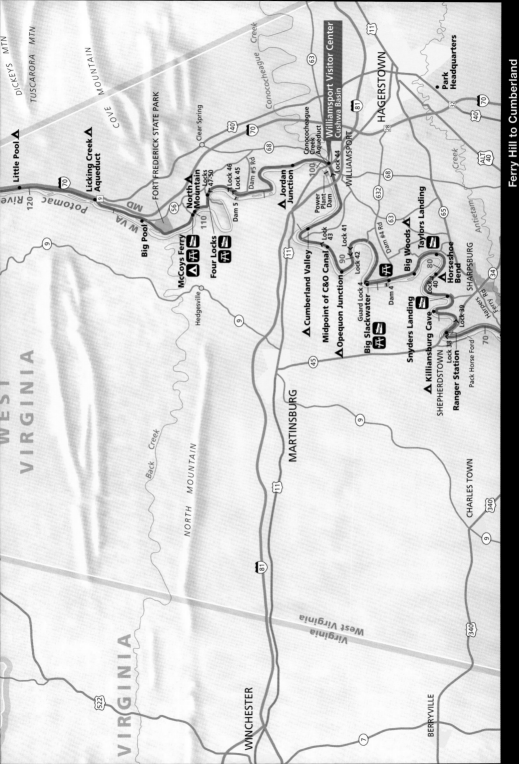

Ferry Hill to Cumberland

Ferry Hill. Ferry Hill Plantation House overlooks the river high above Lock 38 across from Shepherdstown, **Milepost 73**. The plantation was named for the river ferry here. Canal information is available here.

Killiansburg Cave. One of a series of shallow caves in river cliffs in this area, Killiansburg Cave, **Milepost 75**, served as a refuge for Sharpsburg residents during the Civil War Battle of Antietam.

Snyders Landing and Taylors Landing. River boat ramps make these popular recreation areas, **Milepost 80**. Here the Potomac makes a series of looping bends, the uppermost known as Horseshoe Bend.

Big Slackwater. At this slackwater navigation, boats went out into the river for 3¼ miles. The canal resumes at Lock 41, which functions as an inlet lock. **Note:** Do *not* use the towpath here when the river level is high.

Williamsport. Williamsport (see pages 96 and 97) retains the aura of a canal town, **Milepost 100**. In the summer of 1863, Confederate Gen. Robert E. Lee and his troops crossed the Potomac near here after the Battle of Gettysburg.

Norfolk and Western Railroad bridge. Built in 1923, just one year before a major flood would close the canal for good, this bridge at Williamsport lifted a short section of railroad tracks to allow canal boats to pass.

Conococheague Creek Aqueduct. Mosby's Raiders damaged part of this aqueduct's upper end by blasting during the Civil War, **Milepost 100**.

Locks 45 and 46. Lock 45 is actually a river lock that allowed boats back into the canal after the ½-mile slackwater navigation above Dam 5. Just upstream of Lock 46 the canal widened in a basin that the canal company used for a boat repair operation.

Four Locks. The National Park Service provides a river boat ramp and bulletin board at lock house 49. Locks 47 to 50 occur within a distance of ¼ mile. **Milepost 110.**

Fort Frederick State Park. Fort Frederick was built in 1756, to defend the American frontier during the French and Indian War, **Milepost 112**. British prisoners were detained here during the Revolutionary War. In the Civil War, Union soldiers were based here to protect the canal and railroad. Maryland operates the restored fort, which includes a small museum and offers programs and tours in summer.

Big Pool. Canal engineers created a 1½-mile-long lake here rather than follow the lay of the land, **Milepost 114**. A stop gate functioned as a dam for Big Pool when the canal was drained in winter. This is one of the few watered sections of the canal above Violettes Lock today. Licking Creek Aqueduct lies 2 miles above Big Pool. Another 2½ miles upstream lies the site of Millstone, a village stagecoach stop along the National Road, later U.S. 40, now merged here with I-70.

Little Pool. At Little Pool the canal's engineers created another small lake by siting the towpath on an island, thereby canalizing the small river channel, **Milepost 120**.

Hancock. The National Park Service operates a canal information center with museum exhibits on Main Street in Hancock, **Milepost 125**. There is a river boat ramp here. Tonoloway Creek Aqueduct lies just below the town. Frontier Fort Tonoloway, built here in 1755, was abandoned when Fort Frederick was built in 1756. Hancock was a major stop on the National Road, whose traffic was reduced by railroad competition about 1850. Many boating families wintered in this town full of warehouses.

Round Top Cement Mill lies some 3 miles up the canal.

Dam 6. Dam 6 became the head of canal navigation in 1842 when all work halted for 8 years of scrambling for money to finish the waterway. Confederate troops made several efforts to destroy or disable this feeder dam during the Civil War. Sideling Hill Creek Aqueduct lies 1½ miles upstream.

Little Orleans. Writ large on the frontier history of Western Maryland, Little Orleans lies at the mouth of Fifteen Mile Creek, which the canal crossed on its aqueduct by that name, **Milepost 140.** Little Orleans General Store remains a canal institution now serving local recreationists and hikers and bikers rather than boatmen. There is a river boat ramp here.

Paw Paw Tunnel. Tightly grouped locks 62 to 66 lift the canal to tunnel level, **Milepost 155.** For economy's sake, Lock 65 was omitted. Tunnel (see page 25), river bends, and town across the river are named for the paw paw tree.

Oldtown. Settled by Shawnee Indians in 1692, Oldtown, **Milepost 167,** was chosen for a fortified settlement about 1741 by frontiersman Thomas Cresap. Civil War action here followed a Confederate skirmish against Chambersburg, Pennsylvania.

Evitts Creek Aqueduct. In great disrepair now, Evitts Creek Aqueduct, **Milepost 180,** is the smallest and uppermost of 11 canal aqueducts.

Cumberland. The towpath extended up Wills Creek (see pages 96 and 97). The canal's Cumberland Visitor Center is in the old Western Maryland Railroad Station, which was built in the canal basin, **Milepost 185.** The station building also houses railroad and industrial museums and Allegany County's tourist office.

Turtles sunbathe on a log

A barred owl in winter

A toad reserves judgment
on his photographer

Williamsport: Canal Town

Halfway between Georgetown and Cumberland, Williamsport was the quintessential canal town. Coal helped make it so: much of the coal loaded at Cumberland was destined for two Williamsport dealers—Cushwa and Steffey & Findlay. Canal boats could reach Williamsport as early as 1834 by moving upriver on the slackwater behind Dam No. 4. The canal reached the town the next year, opening a conduit for increased prosperity. The construction of the canal proved a mixed blessing, as a cholera epidemic migrated upstream to Williamsport in 1832. Two years later, rival Irish workers, numbering perhaps 1,000, clashed near the town in bloody battles

that left several dead. Before the canal came, Williamsport had long been a lively river trading port, accessible via the Patowmack Company's river improvements and skirting canals. It was an entrepot for Cumberland Valley produce bound for Georgetown and Alexandria. George Washington had even considered it as a site for the new national capital, but large vessels could not reach a town so far upriver. Its location at a strategic river crossing made it the scene of troop movements and encampments during the Civil War. Stonewall Jackson's soldiers destroyed a section of Dam No. 5 above Williamsport.

Cumberland: Canal Terminus

Cumberland, Maryland, was in the unique position of being the western terminus of the C&O Canal, a stop on the B&O Railroad, and the eastern terminus of the Cumberland Road. In the mid-19th century it was the center of the eastern coal trade and the most important trading city between tidewater and the Ohio River—the "Queen City of the Alleghenies." Cumberland was founded by the Ohio Company in 1749 to tap the trade along the upper Potomac Valley. The completion of the Cumberland Road in 1818 from Cumberland to Wheeling, Virginia (now West Virginia)—the major route from the head of Potomac navigation to the Ohio River—

made Cumberland a regional center of commerce. The canal reached Cumberland in 1850, allowing coal to be shipped east in great quantities. Brought in by rail, the coal was loaded from hopper cars into boats: 10 tons to the car, 12 carloads to the boat. Not only did the canal's main cargo originate in Cumberland, but the town's boatyards also turned out most of the canal boats. Boat crews made about 25 round trips a year from Cumberland, and many spent the winter there, living on their boats. Over the years Cumberland built a solid economic base and, unlike other canal towns, prospered after the canal was gone.

Historic sections of Williamsport retain the atmosphere of the old canal town. An interesting late addition to the canal is the railroad bridge (1923), which lifted tracks over the canal to let boats pass. In the aerial photo, canal aqueduct and a portion of the loading basin are visible.

The National Park Service **Visitor Center** in Cumberland is located in the 1910 Western Maryland Railroad Station. Map shows the canal basins.

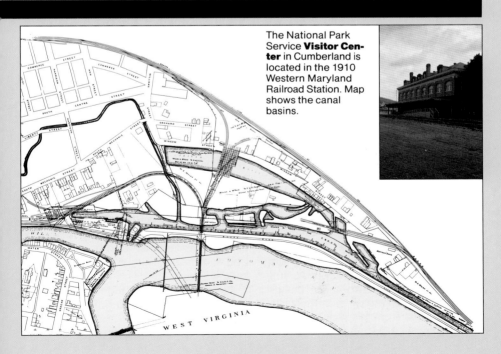

Recreation

A profound pleasure of the C&O Canal is that seeking out its history along its towpath becomes a recreational pursuit in itself. On the canal's unwatered sections, progressive reassertions of nature's claims on its earthen and stone works seem to blend the waterway's cultural and natural histories. Generally, the canal is watered from Georgetown to Violettes Lock, near Seneca, although flooding can disrupt this scheme. Except at Big Pool, Little Pool, and between Town Creek and Oldtown, the rest of the canal is no longer watered.

In this and the following three pages, hiking, biking, canoeing, boating, and fishing opportunities are described. Many other recreational activities are pursued in the park, including walking, jogging, birdwatching, botanizing, and photography. If you have any question about an activity, please see the Management and Safety section on pages 108 and 109, or contact a park office listed on pages 76 and 77.

Hiking. Hiking has been an especially honorable canal pasttime since Justice William O. Douglas organized the trek along its full length that proved crucial to the waterway's eventual preservation. Pleasant hiking conditions—level walking on a carefully prepared surface—are the continuing, inviting legacy of the canal towpath. Originally it was 12 feet wide, built to provide secure footing for the teams of mules that pulled canal boats. For most of its 184.5-mile length the towpath still retains the character of a narrow roadway rather than a trail.

The degree of solitude varies widely with time and place. Weekends, holidays, and vacation times are busiest, especially in the warmer months. Canal use is heaviest from Washington to Seneca, **Mileposts 1-23,** and near Harpers Ferry, **Milepost 60.** The Washington to Seneca stretch often has heavy bicycle traffic. The most remote sections are from Shepherdstown to Dam 4, **Mileposts 70-85,** and from Hancock to North Branch, **Mileposts 125-180.**

For information on where to hike and what conditions to expect, check with the park sources listed on pages 76 and 77. **Through hikers and bikers must check on current camping regulations before planning a trip: camping is restricted to designated areas only.** Availability of approved drinking water sources and legal camping sites varies by seasons and may be affected by flooding. (See below for information about commercial stores.)

Bicycling. You can ride through nature and history on a readily passable, largely level byway free of motorized vehicles. Other qualities that recommend the canal towpath for hiking equally recommended it for bicycling, with some qualifications.

Washouts caused by local or regional flooding may be more of a hazard for bikers than for hikers. A few towpath stretches should routinely be avoided by bikers, such as the upper reaches of Widewater, below Great Falls, **Milepost 13,** where you would have to carry your bicycle over rocky stretches. There, a road above the canal's berm side serves as a bypass. Check with park rangers (see pages 76 and 77) for current conditions along your proposed route. Early spring and fall are the rainier seasons, and mud can slow your progress. You must trade off such considerations against the heat, insects, and increased foot traffic of the summer season.

Note: Cyclists are subject to the caveats and camping restrictions that apply to hikers and all canal users. See Hiking, above, and the information under

Management and Safety on pages 108 and 109 before setting out. In addition, bicyclists must observe the following regulations: Do not exceed 15 mph. Sound your bell or horn when approaching within 100 feet of other towpath users. Ride single-file and stay to the right unless passing. Yield to pedestrians and horses. Wear a helmet as required by local law.

Bicycle rentals are available at Thompson's Boat Center, Fletcher's Boathouse, and Swains Lock, as shown on the maps at **Mileposts 0, 3, and 16,** respectively.

Through-hiker with laden dog

Canoeing and Boating. Watered sections of the canal between Georgetown and Violettes Lock are popular for canoeing and boating. Big Pool, Little Pool, at **Mileposts 114 and 120,** and a short stretch from Town Creek to Oldtown, **Mileposts 163-167,** are also watered. Novices can learn the finer points of canoe handling free of normal river hazards, which abound on the Potomac River, for example. Flatwater canoeing between locks is restful and provides quiet fishing on widewater stretches of the canal. Canoe rentals are available at Fletcher's Boathouse and Swains Lock. Motorized craft are generally prohibited on the canal.

Cyclists near Dam #3

The National Park Service provides public access boat ramps on the Potomac River at areas indicated on the maps. Various states and private concerns also offer boat ramp facilities along Potomac shores. **Do not attempt to canoe on the Potomac River unless you are an experienced canoeist.** Information regarding river canoeing is available at the Great Falls Visitor Center, **Milepost 14.** Canoeing is specifically discouraged at Great Falls of the Potomac and between Dam 3 just north of Harpers Ferry and the U.S. 340 bridge

Canoeists near Georgetown

downstream from Harpers Ferry, **Milepost 60.** Boating is also hazardous in these areas and should not be attempted when water levels are high, regardless of your expertise. **All boating on the Potomac River is subject to Maryland regulations.** (See the map legends for locating other rapids and hazardous river areas.)

Camping. Camping areas are indicated on the maps in this handbook by two tent symbols. The black tent locates hiker-biker overnight campsites. The white tent within a black shield locates all other campgrounds. **Camping is permitted in designated areas only.** Campsites shown on the maps are operated by the National Park Service. A few State of Maryland and private campgrounds are easily accessible from the canal for hikers and bikers.

Hiker-biker overnight campsites are tenting sites **for overnight use only by hikers and bikers doing long stretches of the canal.** One-night stays only are allowed. These sites occur at approximately 5-mile intervals along the towpath from Horsepen Branch to Evitts Creek (about Mileposts 25 to 180), usually some distance from road access points. The hiker-biker at the Marsden Tract, shown on the map on page 79 at about Milepost 11, requires a free permit that can be obtained from the park ranger at Great Falls (see page 76 for Great Falls area information).

Drive-in camping areas operate on a first-come, first-served basis. They offer primitive facilities and are open from Memorial Day through Labor Day. At Antietam Creek, **Milepost 69,** you park your car on the berm side of the canal and carry your gear and supplies to campsites on the towpath side. **Group camping is allowed only at designated group campgrounds** at the Marsden

Tract, Antietam Creek, and next to Fifteen Mile Creek.

Fishing. The Potomac River and parts of the canal offer anglers both native and introduced game fish. Introduced species are smallmouth and largemouth bass, bluegill sunfish, blue catfish, and rock bass. Brown and rainbow trout are stocked in some of the mountain tributaries. Native fish include black and white crappies, chain pickerel, yellow perch, pumpkinseed, white cat, channel cat, and American eel. Brook trout are native to a few headwater streams.

More a place for contemplation than exciting fishing, the canal nevertheless contains fish. Blue and channel catfish, carp, several sunfish species, and pickerel predominate, with here and there occasional bass. Watered sections of the canal are from Georgetown to Seneca, **Mileposts 0-23;** at Big Pool and Little Pool, **Mileposts 113** and **120;** and a short stretch from Town Creek to Oldtown, **Mileposts 163-167.** Widewater, just below Great Falls on the canal, provides good fishing for several species, including bass, **Milepost 14.** Big and Little Pools, **Mileposts 113** and **120,** offer the most variety, including white and yellow perch and crappie along with the more ubiquitous species.

On the Potomac, fishing changes from one stretch of the river to another. Deep-water bass fishing can be had near Shepherdstown, **Milepost 70.** Near Harpers Ferry the river below Dam 3 is good for catfish and bass, **Milepost 60.** On the river near Lock 34 a deep channel offers good crappie fishing in spring and fall, **Milepost 61.** Whites Ferry offers good crappie fishing, too, sometimes even in winter because effluent from the power plant at Dickerson warms the river water, **Milepost 35.** Carp and catfish fishing is good near the Point of Rocks Bridge, **Milepost 48,** and at the mouth of the Monocacy, **Milepost 42.**

At Chain Bridge, below Little Falls, hickory shad and herring swarm by the thousands in spring, and other species can be caught through the summer and fall, **Milepost 4.** Ask at Fletcher's Boathouse for information about fishing the river nearby.

April weekends find anglers lined up on the river near Chain Bridge to catch, often by the bucketsful, herring and shad fighting their way upriver in the annual spring spawning run. Alewife, blueback herring, hickory shad, and American shad spawn in freshwater at the head of tidal sections of many East Coast rivers. So do white perch and striped bass. Little Falls, **Milepost 6,** constitutes an obstacle that concentrates them in a narrow channel convenient for fishing.

Anglers go after smallmouth bass as the premier game fish. September and October are the best months for smallmouth, although they can be caught throughout the warmer months. Bass haunt riffles and rapids, feeding on aquatic insects. Bass fishing is at its finest on the Potomac between the Monocacy River and Hancock, **Mileposts 42-125.** Most popular is the stretch between Brunswick and Knoxville, **Mileposts 55-57.** However, President Herbert H. Hoover preferred to do his bass fishing below Little Orleans. **Milepost 140.** President Grover Cleveland liked to fish near Edwards Ferry, **Milepost 30.**

Fishing in the canal and river comes under Maryland regulations. A license is required for fishing in the canal and in the river above Little Falls.

At a hiker-biker campsite

A young angler tries his luck

Crosscountry skiing

As the Potomac River courses through valleys, ridges, and piedmont hills, it nurtures along its borders plants and animals not found in the surrounding highlands. Just as settlers used the river as a trade artery, plant and animal species have migrated along its corridor: downstream from the highlands, upstream from the lowlands to the south. A climate similar to that of the Coastal Plain extends up the river into the hills above Washington. In the mountainous regions farther north, the temperature in the river valley may be several degrees higher than on the nearby ridges. Species from the south will follow the valley for as long as it provides hospitable niches, significantly extending their range. In effect, they make a long, narrow incursion into a foreign environment, protected by the river valley. The river itself is responsible for the southerly movement of species, usually plants. Of the millions of seeds that float down the river, a very few are deposited on protected patches of fertile soil where they can germinate. Animals, too, follow the river southward, using the gaps cut by the river through the steep ridges. The river provides a way for plants and animals to overcome obstacles of climate and terrain that would otherwise have blocked their migration.

Southerly Migrators
Smooth green snake
Northern white cedar
Wake-robin
Moss pink
Brown wood rat
Black-capped chickadee

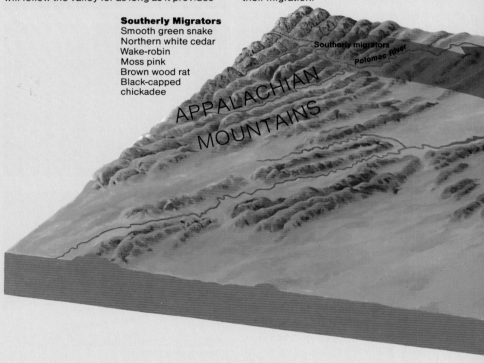

Extended Ranges
The distance that some species extend their ranges along the river is considerable, as shown on the map. The gradual elevation gradient of the river valley creates the gradual temperature gradient that allows the northern movement of willow oak, Carolina chickadee, and mud turtle. Wake-robin and moss-pink migrate south to find sustaining environments on the river's cool limestone slopes and Great Falls' rocky cliffs. Mountainous hemlock and rosebay rhododendron can be found along the river as far south as Washington. In some cases, the ranges of two closely related species from different environments meet along the river. Because these species, such as the northern smooth green snake and southern rough green snake, have adapted to different climates but compete for the same kind of food and living space, their ranges overlap little.

American eel

Each spring, white suckers, shad, and herring push upstream on their annual spawning run. After spawning in the freshwater above the tidal head, they return to the sea. Eels swim from far upriver to their spawning grounds off Bermuda, almost 1,000 miles away. The young return to begin the cycle anew.

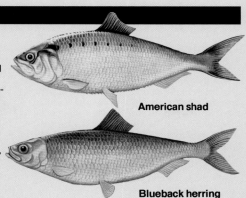

American shad

Blueback herring

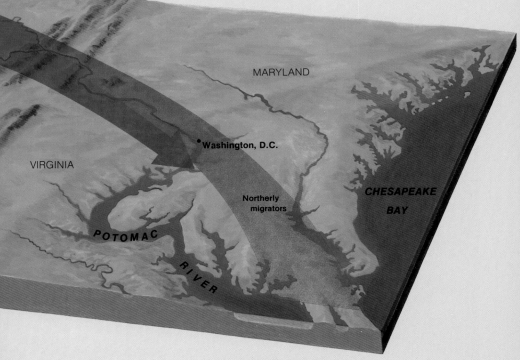

MARYLAND

•Washington, D.C.

VIRGINIA

Northerly migrators

CHESAPEAKE BAY

POTOMAC RIVER

Northerly Migrators
Rough green snake
Willow oak
Black vulture
River birch
Mud turtle
Carolina chickadee

The Floodplain Forest

Along much of the length of the C&O, the visitor encounters a distinct environmental zone lying between the canal and the Potomac—the river floodplain. Most of this floodplain is narrow and remains relatively unchanged. Several characteristics distinguish the floodplain from the surrounding area: the water table is high, there is little runoff, and its water-holding silt loam is rich in limestone and calcium, providing a moist and fertile habitat for a variety of plant and animal species. Box elder, hackberry, and green ash are among the trees that thrive on the floodplain. Many of these species are successional, occupying open ground until larger, shade-tolerant trees shut out the sunlight. While the floodplain provides a rich habitat for many species, it can turn deadly when many young animals are drowned during floods.

1 Carolina chickadee	12 Two-lined salamander
2 Raccoon	13 Copperhead
3 White-tailed deer	14 Wood duck
4 Red-headed woodpecker	15 Turkey vulture
5 Beaver	16 Pileated woodpecker
6 Gray squirrel	17 Red fox
7 Striped skunk	18 Black rat snake
8 White-footed mouse	19 Wake robin (trillium)
9 Pickerel frog	20 Opossum
10 Jack-in-the-pulpit	21 Spring peeper
11 American toad	22 Eastern box turtle

At a bend in a river, the stronger current on the outer side eats away at the bank. At the same time, the slower water on the inner side deposits silt there. The bend thus migrates, leaving behind point-bar deposits that form floodplains. The upper terraces are old floodplains, left behind as the river cut deeper.

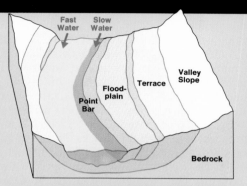

Fast Water

Slow Water

Valley Slope

Terrace

Flood-plain

Point Bar

Bedrock

Floodplain trees have evolved ways to cope with their stressful environment. Their roots can tolerate inundation. Their shallow, widespread root systems anchor them firmly yet stay above waterlogged soil. The seeds of the silver maple, sycamore, and black willow remain viable after floating on water for long periods.

American hackberry

River birch

American elm

Sycamore

Cottonwood

P.A. TOPPER

Interpretive Activities and Community Programs

Interpretive activities sponsored by the National Park Service operate out of the canal visitor and information centers shown on the maps in this handbook. Activities include guided walks, talks, slide shows, canal boat rides, and ranger-led bicycling excursions. They are listed below according to the visitor or information center where they occur or where you can get information about them.

Georgetown. Topping the list of activities at Georgetown is a ride on the reconstructed canal boat *The Georgetown.* Your boat's crew of costumed interpreters expertly handles the boat and its mules and entertains you with canal lore and period music. Boat rides leave from Lock 3—under genuine mule power—and lock through a lift lock. Georgetown's many historic facades on the canal enhance this trip back in time. Canal Boat Rides on page 76 tells about ticket sales, schedules, and seasons. Also at Georgetown, conducted walks and talks explore the character of Georgetown's waterfront before, during, and after its canal era. See the Georgetown area canal phone number on page 76.

Great Falls. Boat rides are also offered at Great Falls, Maryland, with costumed interpreters. Canal Boat Rides on page 76 tells about ticket sales, schedules, and seasons. In the Great Falls Tavern (see pages 88 and 89) you can see the museum displays of historic canal artifacts, buy maps and books, and find out about interpretive activities. Join a guided nature walk along the towpath to learn about local flowers and birds, fish, and other wildlife. See the Great Falls area canal phone number on page 76.

Williamsport. Just off U.S. 11 in the Cushwa Basin is the park's Williamsport Visitor Center. The basin was a major coal market and distribution center. The old Cushwa warehouse has exhibits on canal life and commerce. Interpretive programs here include hikes and bike rides and lock demonstrations at Lock 44. For Williamsport area canal information call 301-582-0813, V/TDD. Maps and books about the canal, Potomac River and Williamsport area are sold at the Williamsport Visitor Center.

Hancock. On its Main Street in Hancock, the park's Hancock Visitor Center offers an exhibit about life on the canal, **Milepost 125.** Posterized historic photographs and original artifacts convey a sense of the canal's working years. Part of the exhibit is set up as a canal boat stable, the forward cabin where the off-duty mules were boarded. For Hancock area canal information call 301-678-5463, V/TDD. Maps and books about the canal and Potomac River are sold at the Hancock Visitor Center. See Community Programs (below) for more Hancock area information.

Cumberland. The park's Cumberland Visitor Center houses an exhibit of canal history and life. Included in this center are exhibits on the construction of the canal, boat building, and coal mining as well as parts of a reproduction canal boat that show how canallers lived. The National Park Service Cumberland Visitor Center occupies the first floor of the 1910 Western Maryland Railroad Station, which is operated by the Canal Place Authority. Wayside exhibits outside the visitor center explain what the canal was like here in Cumberland, its western terminus. Parts of the historic canal basin are being rewatered. Most evidence of the canal here, however, has been obliterated by development and flood control projects.

Interpretive activities here include orientation talks on the canal's history and present-day canal activities. These include hiking and backpacking, biking, crosscountry skiing, and canoeing. Here you can also get information on canal activities that take place below Cumberland. For example, tours are conducted through the Paw Paw Tunnel (see map on pages 92 and 93). Information about these is also posted on the bulletin board at the Paw Paw Tunnel area parking lot, **Milepost 155.** A flashlight is recommended for use inside the tunnel.

Maps and books about the canal and its Cumberland environs are sold at the visitor center. For Cumberland area canal information call 301-722-8226, V/TDD.

Community Programs. The National Park Service is also a partner in programs that blend canal history and festivals and art fairs. **CanalFest** in Cumberland in July celebrates the city's diverse transportation history: contact the Canal Place Authority or Cumberland information (above). Hancock's **Canal Apple Festival** on a fall weekend celebrates the harvest season and the canal. For information contact the Hancock Lions Club, town office, or the Hancock area canal information (above). **Williamsport Canal Days,** in late summer is an old timey town festival featuring crafts people in a fairgrounds atmosphere near where many canal boat captains and their families lived. For information about this event contact the Williamsport town hall or General Canal Information on page 76.

Canal boaters in Georgetown

Nature walk near Monocacy Aqueduct

Backpackers at Paw Paw Tunnel

Management and Safety Considerations

Many management concerns and safety tips are given under the descriptions of activities and facilities throughout Part 3 of this handbook. Please read the appropriate entry before undertaking any activity. Following are general information on the canal's management and additional safety tips intended to protect both you and the canal.

Driving Tips and Vehicle Security. Many canal parking areas and access roads in the Greater Washington Metropolitan Area lead onto busy streets and highways. Be extremely cautious about city traffic in such situations. Some canal access roads in rural areas are narrow, winding, and tortuous. When wet they can be treacherous. Drive defensively and err on the side of caution. **Motor vehicles—including motorcycles, trail bikes, and snowmobiles—are prohibited on the canal towpath except where authorized access to river boat ramps may cross it. Horsedrawn vehicles are also prohibited on the towpath.** Park vehicles in designated areas only. Do not block emergency access gates to the C&O Canal towpath. Vehicles in violation will be towed at the owner's expense. Always lock your car when you leave it unattended and store valuables in the trunk or otherwise out of sight.

Pets. Pets must be on a leash no more than 6 feet long and must be under physical restraint at all times.

Respect Wildlife. Keep a respectful distance from all animals to avoid disturbing their natural routines, especially when taking pictures. Larger animals such as bear and deer are quick, powerful, and unpredictable. Getting too close can result in serious injury. Smaller animals such as chipmunks, squirrels, and turtles—especially snapping turtles—can bite and may carry diseases. Periodic outbreaks of rabies can occur. **Feeding wild animals is prohibited.** Be alert for poisonous snakes, including copperheads; snakes and other animals are protected by law. Do not molest or harm them.

Poison Ivy and Poison Oak. Know how to recognize plant irritants. Ask at any information center.

Hiking and Bicycling. Local or regional flooding may inundate or wash out portions of the towpath. When this occurs, hikers and bicyclists should turn back. Night travel is not recommended. Bring drinking water.

Picnicking. You may picnic anywhere along the canal. Please leave the area in as good or better condition than you found it. **Fires are permitted only where fireplaces are provided.** Drink water only from approved water sources. River, canal, stream, and spring waters must be considered polluted.

Camping. See page 100. For complete regulations contact an information center— see pages 76 and 77.

No Swimming. Swimming and wading in canal waters are prohibited.

Guns and Hunting Prohibited. No type of gun, including BB guns and air rifles, is permitted in the park. Hunting is prohibited in the park. Hunters with unloaded and cased weapons may cross park property to reach adjacent hunting lands. Camping in the park for the purpose of establishing a hunting base is not allowed.

Violations and Unusual Circumstances. Please report all violations of regulations and any unusual circumstances you may encounter to a park ranger. See pages 76 and 77 for the appropriate telephone numbers.

Land Ownership. Please respect adjoining private property and agricultural uses. Leave gates open or closed as you find them.

River Safety. Never underestimate the power and treachery of the Potomac River. Even strong swimmers may become exhausted and drown in apparently gentle waters. Please stay away from the river's edge and closely watch and control your children at all times. After rainstorms areas of the riverbank can be extremely slippery with heavy muds. Other bank areas may be undercut and weakened so that your body weight may send them—and you— falling into the river. Often the river plunges to significant depth right at its bank, too. **Please see warnings under Canoeing and Boating on pages 98 and 99.** Particularly avoid river use in the areas designated as hazardous in the legends on the maps in this handbook. Remember that personal flotation devices are required by law. Wear yours properly fastened.

Horseback Riding. For information about regulations governing the use of horses on the canal, please write to the park headquarters address on page 76.

Recreational Sites Hours. Developed recreational sites are located at Four Locks, Big Slackwater, Nolands Ferry, Great Falls, and Carderock. All close at dark.

Further Reading

The nonprofit Parks and History Association, P.O. Box 40929, Washington, DC 20016 (telephone 202-472-3083), sells books, maps, and other publications about the canal in support of the interpretive and management programs of the park. Items may be purchased at most canal information centers or by mail. Write for a free list of titles. The following books may also be of interest.

Bacon-Foster, Corra. *Early Chapters in the Development of the Patomac [sic] Route to the West.* New York: Burt Franklin, 1971 (reprint of 1912 edition).

Gutheim, Frederick. *The Potomac.* New York: Rinehart & Company, Inc., 1949.

Hahn, Thomas F. *The C&O Canal: An Illustrated History.* Shepherdstown, W.Va.: American Canal and Transportation Center, 1981.

Hahn, Thomas F. *The Chesapeake & Ohio Canal: Pathway to the Nation's Capital.* Metuchen, N.J., The Scarecrow Press, Inc., 1984.

Hahn, Thomas F. *Towpath Guide to the C&O Canal: Georgetown Tidelock to Cumberland.* Shepherdstown, W.Va.: American Canal and Transportation Center, 1985.

Kytle, Elizabeth. *Home on the Canal.* Washington, D.C.: Seven Locks Press, 1983.

Mason-Dixon Council, Boy Scouts of America. *184 Miles of Adventure: Hiker's Guide to the C&O Canal.* P.O. Box 2133, Hagerstown, Md. 21742, 1983.

Sanderlin, Walter S. *The Great National Project.* Baltimore, Md.: The Johns Hopkins Press, 1946.

Index

☆GPO:2004—497-153/60515 Reprint 2004
Printed on recycled paper

The National Park Service expresses its appreciation to all those persons who made the preparation and production of this handbook possible. All photos and artwork not credited below come from the files of the National Park Service; some may be restricted against commercial reproduction.

B&O Railroad Museum 72 horse painting by H. D. Stitt
Greg Beaumont 17, 31 photo, 67, 90 Harpers Ferry, 95 turtles and toad, 101 all
Columbia Historical Society 9 seal
Cumberland (Md.) Department of Community Development 63 top
Donald Demers artwork on 32-39, 52-55
David Guiney 99 cyclists
T. Thomas Swiftwater Hahn Collection 61 Hancock
Historical Society of Washington, D.C., 82 boat traffic
Elizabeth Kytle 48, 49
Robert Lautman covers, 2-5, 8, 11, 16, 18-19, 25-27, 74-75, 77 top and bottom, 81 top, 88-89, 107 top
Library of Congress 35 Leonardo, 62 bottom, 69 bottom, 82-83 map, L'Enfant's plan, and aqueduct
Maryland Historical Society 12-13
Steven Patricia artwork 56-57
Savage/Fogarty Real Estate, Inc. 82 Alexandria lock
Richard Schlecht artwork 68-69, 70-71 furnace, 90-91
Smithsonian Institution 62 top and middle, 69 castle, 96 bottom
Patricia Topper 30-31 block diagram, artwork 102-105 except floodplain diagram
Ken Townsend 71 implements
Washington and Lee University 9 George Washington

Handbook 142

National Park Handbooks are compact introductions
to the great natural and historic places administered
by the National Park Service. They are designed to
promote understanding and enjoyment of the parks.
Each is intended to be informative reading before,
during, and after a park visit. More than 100 titles
are in print. They are sold at parks and can be
purchased by mail from the Superintendent of Docu-
ments, U.S. Government Printing Office, Washington, DC 20402.

Library of Congress Cataloging-in-Publication Data
Chesapeake and Ohio Canal.
(Official national park handbook; 142)
Bibliography: p.
Includes index.
1. Chesapeake and Ohio Canal National Historical
Park—Guide-books. 2. Chesapeake and Ohio
Canal (Md. and Washington, D.C.)—History. I.
United States. National Park Service. Division of
Publications. II. Series: Handbook (United States.
National Park Service. Division of Publications);
142.
F187.C47C47 1989 975 88-25305